CREAM PEAS ON TOAST

Comfort Food for Norwegian-Lutheran Farm Kids (and Others)

Janet Letnes Martin

and

Suzann (Johnson) Nelson

CARAGANA PRESS

CARAGANA PRESS
Box 396
HASTINGS, MN 55033

Copyright © 1994 by Janet Letnes Martin
and Suzann (Johnson) Nelson

Printed in the United States of America

Published by Caragana Press
Box 396, Hastings, Minnesota 55033

Library of Congress Catalog Card Number 94-068431

ISBN 0-961-3437-9-6

FIRST EDITION

Photo credits:

Cover photo by Paulstad Communications

St. Joseph's School, Grand Rapids, Minnesota (page 53)

Minnesota Historical Society, St. Paul Pioneer Press (page 55 & 94)

Dino Sassi, *Foto; Forlag: Fra Meg til deg kart*, A.S. Oslo (page 129)

Sven Johansson, *Lima bortam manna minne* (page 155)

Dedication

This handy dandy Book is dedicated not only to
Norwegian-Lutheran Farm Kids, but also to:
Norwegian-Lutheran Wannabes,
Swedish Lutherans, Danish Lutherans,
ALC-ers, ELC-ers, LCA-ers,
Augustana Synod Lutherans,
Wisconsin Synod Lutheran Kids,
German & Missouri Synod Lutheran Kids,
Free-ers & other Renegade Breakaways,
Folks who remember
The Black Hymnal & THE CONCORDIA,
"Feast in Paradise-ers"
& "Strengthen for Thy service be-ers,"
and Others who Grew Up
before the last two or three Lutheran Mergers
and are Current ELCA-ers
and
Finnish-Lutherans (& Socialists),
Covenants Kids (Mission & Swedish),
Wesleyan & Easy-Study Confirmation Methodists,
Episcopalians, Presbyterians, Dutch Reformers,
Congregationalists, UCC-ers,
Pentecostals (from Karlstad, Minnesota, & Elsewhere),
Baptists, Nazarenes, United Brethren (& Cistern)
and (Brandon, Minnesota, Catholics)
& Other Holy Roman Catholics who ate Fish and
Cream Peas on Toast on Fridays,
and Small Town Kids,
Cousins from the Suburbs and from California,
and Rook Players.

Acknowledgments

Mange tusen takk to:

Our Friend Sarah the Gardener and Shucker,

Genevieve Dodge of Minneapolis who was gracious enough to let us photograph the Peas she Canned in 1934, and to Jim Klobuchar for alerting his readers to the existence of Genevieve's Peas,

William W. Wallwork III for letting us reuse a favorite radio jingle,

People who were good enough to give us their Church Centennial Books, especially First Lutheran Church in St. Paul, Minnesota, East and West Zion in the Benson, Minnesota, area, and Grace Lutheran in Erskine, Minnesota,

Our PK model K.D.L., the Good Sport who keeps us flying high,

Our PK model who is clinging to Cleng,

Carroll's Antiques of Hastings who let us photograph their Toaster because since The War, all our Relatives have become so Fancy and Modern that they threw out the Flip-Down-the-Sides Family Toasters even though they were perfectly good still,

the Roys next door who have one mean Pressure Cooker,

and Carol Frick, our rock in Rockford, who performed miracles on a crazy layout of a crazy text written by two goofy women.

A Note to Readers

To Our Former Teachers

In case any of you are reading this Handy Dandy Book, we would like to explain that you taught us well—especially grammar. However, in keeping with the Tradition of many of our general readers and Relatives, you will find that the important words—especially nouns—are capitalized. These are Comfort words like Services, Congregation, Bread; words for White Foods or things that come from a Cow; words related to God, Religion, Country, or White; and words for staples such as Lard or Fat.

Sometimes other parts of speech are also capitalized if they are really important: Moral Decay, Hot as in Hot Meal, Wholesome Wife, Normal, etc.

Sometimes verbs are important too—verbs like "To Turn," "Puttin' Up," and "Makin' Do."

Sometimes articles are capitalized in phrases like The Mrs., The Wife, etc.

Geography and Weather were important to Rural Norwegian-Lutherans. These words, the most important ones, are capitalized: Snow, Sea, Prairie, etc.

You will note that words referring to body parts are NOT capitalized. These were not important words. Neither were words related to High-Falutin' stuff—words like hero and money.

Really awful words like sex and dancing and loose and divorce are in smaller-case letters, as they should be.

To Our General Readers

By the time you put this Book down, you'll be speaking with somewhat of a Brogue. This will be temporary, but it will help you Dig up Memories of former words, actions and Friends. Unlike the temporary Brogue, we hope the

Memories will be permanent, and that they will multiply as you Work your way through this Handy Dandy Book.

We speak in the vernacular, so we write in it too. Along with Memories, we also Dig colloquialisms and Potatoes.

To Politically Correct Yuppies and Book Critics

Of course we know that it is grammatically and politically correct to say "These mash well" instead of "These mush good" or "He understood different ethnic groups quite well" instead of "He understood half-breeds really good." We weren't born yesterday, you know! You'll just have to put up with this. You'll live, and maybe you'll learn something too!

Contents

Introduction

No one knows for sure what kind of Pea Brain invented Cream Peas on Toast* or where the idea of Cream Peas on Toast originated, but there are some theories, that's for sure.

This Book contains not only theories about the origin of the extremely popular and Comfort-inducing Cream Peas on Toast, but also accompanying etiquette (the Do's & Don'ts of Cream Peas on Toast), Recipes, and Occasions when one should and shouldn't Serve it, etc.—sort of the Who, What, When, Where and How Come, Then of Cream Peas on Toast.

There are several for-sure facts about Cream Peas on Toast:

1) Most everyone who likes Peas really likes Cream Peas on Toast,
2) Cream Peas on Toast always conjures up good Memories and Nice Thoughts,
3) Cream Peas was always Served on Town (Bought*en*) Bread; never on Homemade Bread,
4) There are times, even Today, when only Cream Peas on Toast will do!

---

*The correct way to say this is probably "Cream*ed*" Peas on Toast, but the "*ed*" is silent like the "*p*" in pneumonia; hence, the correct pronunciation and spelling of this delicacy is Cream Peas on Toast.

Theories About the Origin

# of Cream Peas on Toast

1

THEORIES ABOUT THE ORIGIN OF CREAM PEAS ON TOAST

N O ONE knows for sure where the idea of Cream Peas on Toast came from, but there are some theories. Some of them don't amount to a Hill of Beans, but here goes…

Something old,
Something new,
Something green,
Something grew!

The Le Sueur Immigrant Theory

Some Folks said that maybe when the Norwegian-Lutherans who had earlier moved from Spring Grove, Wisconsin, into Goodhue County in Minnesota were migrating farther North and West, they found a lot of Peas growing around the Le Sueur area that the Grasshoppers had jumped over.

The Immigrants had never eaten Peas before, but they thought that if the Good Lord had caused the Grasshoppers to leave the Peas alone, it was surely a Sign from Above that these Peas were for the Norwegians and that they better not disappoint the Creator.

Yet, Norwegians have always been a little reluctant to try new and different Things, so they decided it would be best if they mixed them with something more Familiar. This idea is similar to the practice of having both Crosses and dragon heads on top of Stave Churches, or keeping the Red Hymnals in the Church Basement when the New Green Ones came for upstairs in the Main Sanctuary—slowly bring in something new without discarding The Old completely.

Well, being Thrifty and hungry, the Immigrants picked the Peas near Le Sueur and mixed some Flour with Milk from Bessie, who was tied to the oxcart. Being Thrifty and hungry, they ate it all up thinking: This isn't so bad, then! Just like Manna from Heaven for The Wanderers.

Besides, they were afraid to say what they really thought because they were Norwegian-Lutherans, and because they had heard stories about giants—Colorful Trolls, Green Giants—lurking in the area, and they weren't so sure they wanted to deal with them.

---

*I NØDEN SPISER
FANDEN FLUER !*
tr. In times of need,
the devil eats flies!

The Depression Invention Theory

In June in about 1931, Cora and Knut, who lived on the Homeplace, were having a tough time making ends meet, but they knew they'd just have to Make Do *(see next year's Book from Caragana Press called* Makin' Do!*),* so they didn't waste a Thing and used up what they had.

Cora, who came from a large Family, had always had to fend for herself so she was kind of clever and had a knack for experimenting, even though she did grow up Norwegian-Lutheran and knew that the Tried and True was best.

The story goes that she had some paste *(the Flour and water kind made in a zinc Jar lid and stirred with a Toothpick)* left over from a Father's Day card made out of Pressed Flowers and Wax Paper that she was making for Knut. She surely didn't want to waste the paste, but it seemed like so little to save. Yet, she knew she shouldn't be wasteful, so she added more water until she had enough paste worth saving.

Well, by then it was getting late. Knut would soon be coming in from Chores and she knew her Main Job was to cook a Hot Meal for Her Man, but she had wasted so much time on the card, and now she had wasted so much Flour and water, that she was really feeling bad.

Besides, it had been so Hot after Services and Noon Dinner, that she hadn't taken time to Do the Dishes and now she had only one Kettle Clean. She grabbed a pint of Peas left over from the year before and threw it in the Kettle and dumped the paste in with it.

She was just about frantic now, but she knew she had to

Make Do and Make Do soon. She added some Milk and some more Flour and pretty soon she had a nice looking stew. But she knew that Knut needed more than that so she grabbed a loaf of Bread and the rest, they say, is history.

The World War II Theory

The World War II theory is a little more believable than either the Le Sueur or Depression theories.

Pearl and Oliver Jensrud got engaged just before Oliver was sent Overseas. Pearl worried a lot, but kept real busy while he was gone. Then right after V-E Day, Oliver came Home—just in time for the Alfalfa. He looked so nice in his Uniform and Pearl was so proud of him.

Well, they got hitched after Fall Harvest and as the years went by, Pearl grew even more proud that Oliver had Served his Country. She wanted their children—Sylvia, Jerry, Margaret and Darrell—to learn about what a hero their Father had been and she wanted to help Oliver remember, too. So every year on Decoration Day, after the Parade of Vets

who were in the Big One, the WWII Vets, the Gold Star Mothers, and the combination Junior and Senior High School Summer Band to the Cemetery, Pearl fixed a Special Meal. *(If you don't know what Decoration Day is, see page 29 in* CREAM AND BREAD.*)*

Not wanting to waste a good piece of meat to Cream by chipping it in pieces like the Army had done, Pearl picked and cooked some Very Early June Peas that she had planted along-side the Potatoes on Good Friday. She mixed this with White Sauce and Served it over Toast to Oliver and the kids.

This became a Tradition the Jensrud Family looked forward to all Winter. They knew that on Decoration Day Mom would again unpack her White Shoes, Dad would again march in the Parade with the other Vets, and at Suppertime they'd all have Cream Peas on Toast—a reminder of what Oliver had Gone Through.

The Young Seminarian's Wife Theory

Some say Cream Peas on Toast is really City Food for Norwegian-Lutheran Farmers and that this Meal really took off in the early '50s when Things were looking good. Farm Bureau members in the Midwest wore I LIKE IKE buttons and were Puttin' Up new Silos and remodeling the Homeplace, and City Cousins were inventing Suburbs. People were basically in a good mood, until some City Folk just got too High Falutin'. If you listened to the Farm Report on 'CCO you could Sense there was tension brewing in the air between City Folks and Farmers. *(Even though almost everyone had a radio now, some felt that the announcers still didn't read the Hog Report nearly enough times, especially on WDAY in Fargo-Moorhead.)*

(A catchy tune heard on Barn radios. Sing along while doing the Morning Milking.)

There's a car for you & a truck there too—
At W.W. Wallworks.
And the price is fair & you're welcome there—
At W.W. Wallworks.

Hey there folks, now don't go 'way,
Listen to what I have got to say—
There's a car for you & a truck there too—
At W.W. Wallworks.

The worst was when young Pastor Tryggve Ynggve got Called to Serve Norunga Lutheran and brought his new Wife, Mary Lou, along! Pastor Ynggve had grown up on a Farm by Blue Earth and he was as Down-to-Earth as can be, but His Mrs. had spent her High School years in Hopkins and she was City through and through. She had even been a candidate for the Raspberry Festival Queen and somewhere in the back of her mind she still thought she was something. The Norwegian-Lutherans around Norunga tried to be nice and polite to the Young Seminarian's Wife, but it wasn't always so easy. She wore a Housecoat instead of a Housedress and Scuffs instead of Wedgies and didn't care if she still had them on after 8:00 in the Morning. *(She even wore show-off clip-on earrings and lipstick on Sundays when Communion was Served.)* When the Larson Boy went to the Parsonage to tell the Pastor that Mrs. Bye was poorly, there she was, the Young Seminarian's Wife, coming to the door at 8:15 with her hair in Pincurls and her Housecoat and Scuffs on. *(She couldn't have been ill because she wasn't even showing yet!)*

By the time the Congregation had started to recover from that, the Young Seminarian's Wife pulled another one! She decided to invite the Council President Bernhard Loftness and His Mrs. and Organist Agnes Thorsrud and Her Man for brunch! Of course, the Loftnesses and the Thorsruds had to be told that brunch was a cross between Breakfast and Lunch and that, in Hopkins, People ate brunch on Sundays.

They knew that they couldn't say no, so even when Mary Lou told them to "Come and eat about 11," all they could do was smile and say, "*Ja*. Thanks, then." They didn't dare ask her what time the Ynggves had Dinner! *(Between Breakfast and Lunch for the Loftnesses and Thorsruds would be somewhere around 8:30—between Breakfast at 7:00 and Lunch at 10:00— and a Meal "about 11" would come awfully close to Noon Dinner).*

Well, they went to the Ynggves after 9:30 Services were over. Mrs. Loftness thought to herself that it was good it was Sunday because at least Mrs. Ynggve would be dressed "by about 11" and that the Parsonage would be picked up too.

The Young Seminarian's Wife Served a brunch, all right. She Served Toast and then, of all Things, she put Cream Peas on top of it. She said she had learned how to make it in Home Ec in High School in Hopkins.

As the Loftnesses and the Thorsruds looked at the White Sauce and then at the young Pastor and His Wife, the Cream Peas almost took on a Spiritual Aura. It was White like Purity and *Sankta Lucia* Gowns and Confirmation Robes. It was green like the Trinity Stoles and the Holy, Holy, Holy Altar Cloth. The Loftnesses and Thorsruds just ate it and didn't say much.

Both Mrs. Loftness and Mrs. Thorsrud were relieved when the Ynggves moved after a year to a bigger Church in the County Seat, and a semi-retired Minister, who knew how to do Things the Right Way and who had been a Missionary in China, was Called to Serve at Norunga Lutheran in the Country.

Clever Corrine,
the County Agent's WifeTheory

Another likely theory about the origin of Cream Peas on Toast is a most popular one. It is called the County Agent's Wife theory. In 1954, Walter and Corrine Knutsvig and Family moved to a small Farm by Alexandria, the County Seat. Walter had gone to the University on the GI Bill and, although he was in his middle 30s, he had landed his first Real Job: Extension Agent for a whole County.

Both Corrine and Walter had grown up on a Farm so they fit right in. Corrine was a 4–H Leader and a good one, too. Even though they had spent some time in The Cities, they were both real Down-to-Earth still.

Of course, because they were used to driving in The Cities, they thought nothing of going there for the State Fair. Well, one year when they were at the State Fair, the same year Corrine got her Veg-o-Matic, it Rained a lot so they spent a Good Deal of time in the 4–H Buildings and watching the demonstrations under the Grandstand. *(It Rained so much that they only spent about two hours on Machinery Hill that year).*

Corrine never could remember where she saw the demonstration of Cream Peas on Toast—under the Grandstand where the new Things are, or in the nutrition division of the 4–H Building. It doesn't much matter. Anyway, when Corrine got Home she volunteered to do the next demonstration at the Happy Homemakers' Club. She borrowed some of Walter's pamphlets from the University and prepared a little talk to go along with her demonstration of Cream Peas on Toast. The September Meeting of the Happy Homemakers' Club was well attended, with all the kids back in School and all that.

Corrine did such a Nice Job. She talked about the importance of Balanced Meals and that children can be taught to eat vegetables if their Moms are very clever. Corrine said Cream Peas on Toast was really a one-step, one-stop nutritious Meal you didn't have to kill yourself making. She said that the Family would get:

- Grains and Cereals in the Bread Portion,
- Dairy from the Cream Portion, and
- Green Vegetables in the form of Peas.

She suggested that the Moms Toast the Bread to make it Special, and if they Served it with a Side of Spam and some Rhubarb Sauce, they'd have a complete Meal. It was a good way to provide a Hot Meal on Sunday Night without much

Fuss. And making Cream Peas and Toast didn't heat up the Kitchen. Pretty soon there were many clever Moms in the County and the kids were eating well without even knowing it. That Corrine was a good one!

Apparently whole Homemakers' Clubs were part of this Mid-western conspiracy. Norwegian-Lutheran Farm kids and others from Minnesota, the Dakotas, Iowa, Illinois, Indiana, Kansas, Missouri, Wyoming, Montana, Nebraska and Wisconsin grew up loving Cream Peas on Toast and being Healthy and Wholesome. This was really important so that Ringworm could be kept under control and also because the Salk Polio Vaccine wasn't generally around until 1956.

Mendel,

Mixed
Marriages

and
Recessive
Genes

2

MENDEL, MIXED MARRIAGES AND RECESSIVE GENES

Mendelian Genetics:

READ THIS SECTION ONLY if you are married, about to be married, going to School to be a Horse Doc or are Serious about studying Crop Production. It can get a little embarrassing. Seminarians, Home Canners and Luther League Convention chaperones can skip this chapter.

Many Norwegian-Lutheran Farmers never studied Mendelian Genetics, mainly because it wasn't taught as it had to do with "sexually reproducing species," but also because they didn't have to learn this. They knew how to grow Things without understanding why Things grew. It just wasn't necessary.

However, many Norwegian-Lutheran Families, especially after The War, could have been saved from a lot of embarrassment if they had learned a little about chromosomes and genes.

Gregor Mendel, an Austrian monk, had little in Common with Norwegian-Lutherans except for his obsession with Peas. Mendel found the reason why mixed marriages didn't always Pan Out and he found this by studying the Common Pea. He understood hybrids and half-breeds really good.

Martin Luther, another monk from the same basic area, must have understood this too because he wrote about "punishing children for the sins of the fathers to the third and fourth generations..." and, even though he was a German, he knew that the best Norwegian-Lutherans would "lead a chaste and pure life in thought, word and deed." *(Of course, this was before T.V.)*

Mendel identified chromosome pairs 1 through 22 leaving number 23 for the sex chromosome. Number 23 eventually became XX in females and XY in males. When an egg and sperm united at fertilization *(this doesn't have to do with Cow manure),* the result was a zygote—a glob of 46 chromosomes arranged in 23 pairs with one from each Parent. Genes were found on the chromosomes in the zygote: two genes, one from each Parent.

It's tough to tell where you stand because some genes are stronger *(dominant)*, and some are weaker *(recessive)* and Mendel learned all this from Peas. He spent six years cross-pollinating, replicating, duplicating, reproducing and cloning Peas, but when he was done he had a formula that explained inherited traits.

In other words, there is a formula and scientific explanation for why we are the way we are.

This monk-Pea Stuff can get pretty technical and, besides, it's not so easy to write or talk about it. Just follow the examples to Get the Drift.

The Formula
for Why We Are the Way We Are
Fixations, Traits and Obsessions

Right away you can tell that Norwegian-Lutherans must be full of not-expressed, keep-it-to-yourself genes.

Mendel's Pea Formula

R=Round Pea Parent
r=Wrinkled Pea Parent

	R	r
R	RR	Rr
r	Rr	rr

You can see from this, then, that:

• If a male R stays True to a female R, the result would be RR (Round Peas)
• If a male R fools around with a female r, the result would be Rr (Round Peas)
• If a male r mixes with a female R, the result would be Rr (Round Peas), BUT
• If a male r messes around with a female r, the result would be rr (Wrinkled Peas).

Mendel studied Round Peas and Wrinkled Peas and yellow ones and green ones. (*At least the monks agree with the Lutherans that God loves all colors—red and yellow, black and*

White, etc. He loves them all.) In six years, Mendel invented a lot of Stuff. *(He probably invented Cream Peas on Toast too, but no one is sure.)* However, because Pea Invention Work wasn't an exact science, Mendel had to consider probability. So must you if you are planning to mate.

The goal for Norwegian-Lutherans—as it was for Mendel and in all probability for Martin Luther too—is to have Pure Parents. So you can see, mixed Marriages have the probability of causing trouble. Just remember, the Tried and True is always the best—No Surprises, No Embarrassment—and No Hard Feelings among the Relatives.

What does this have to do with Vikings and Farmers, you may ask? Plenty! Remember the blue-eyed, blond-haired Mandan Indians? Here's how it could work if, for example, a Norwegian who is Blond and likes White Food marries an Italian who is Catholic and Loud.

If the typical traits are:	ITALIANS	NORWEGIANS
	Loud = L	quiet = *l*
	Touchy = T	not touchy = t
	Extrovert = E	introvert = e
	Catholic = C	lutheran = c
	Spicy Food = S	white food = s
	Black Hair = B	blond hair = b

You see then that it is possible and probable that of the offspring:

	L ITALIAN *C*	
l	**L** *l*	**C** *l*
NORWEGIAN		
c	**Lc**	**Cc**

- ¼ could be both Loud and quiet.
- ¼ would be quiet Catholics. *(There are no Pictures of Catholics in our Family albums.)*
- ¼ could be Loud Lutherans. *(See how Serious this can be?)*
- ¼ could be Catholic lutherans. *(In other words, Episcopalian.)*

Examples of Lc's (Loud lutherans)

Norwegian-American Chippendales

Other examples show just how you are taking your chances.

	B ITALIAN *b*	
b	**Bb**	**bb**
NORWEGIAN		
b	**Bb**	**bb**

- You have ½ a chance that the kids will have Black hair.
- You have ½ a chance that the kids will have blond hair.

    You just never know.

    If the Italian has Sicilian blood, or if the Norwegian is a Sogning, the traits that are strong in these Coastal riff-raff People move around so just about anything could happen. One just never knows. *(See Girls 3 and 4 in photo.)*

Girls 3 and 4

E ITALIAN *e*

Ee	**ee**	*e*
Ee	**ee**	*e*

NORWEGIAN

• You have ½ of a chance that the offspring will be an Extrovert.

• You have ½ of a chance that the offspring will be an introvert.

Let this be a lesson.

Given all the Valleys in Norway and regions in Italy, it is well to remember where you came from. Then too, it can get really tricky if one considers the Mafia and Quislings. It is possible that even you, you there on the Prairie, could have a Black-haired Extrovert with Illusions of Grandeur who skates in a Bought*en* dress and thinks she's Sonja Henie.

In another Italian genotype:

B ITALIAN *B*		
Bb	**Bb**	*b*
Bb	**Bb**	*b*

NORWEGIAN

You would end up with four Black-haired children and no blonds. (Try to explain that one to your Mother and the *Prest.*)

This all just goes to show that if you are about to stray, you should probably get a genetics test first.

In other examples, it is both possible and probable that of the kids:

• ¼ of them would be both Touchy and untouchy. *(Uncertain.)*

T ITALIAN *B*		
Tt	**Bt**	*t*
Tb	**Bb**	*b*

NORWEGIAN

• ¼ of them would have Black hair and not be touchy. *(This is one of the better configurations.)*

• ¼ would be Touchy blonds. *(In other words, there is a probability of producing a* Floozy *from Hollywood.)*

• ¼ could be Black-blonds. *(These must be brunettes, then.)*

Touchy

and

Untouchy

OR

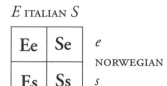

E ITALIAN S

Ee	Se
Es	Ss

e

NORWEGIAN

s

- ¼ could be Extrovert-introverts. *(Close to Danes & Germans.)*
- ¼ could be introverts who like Spicy Foods. *(These People suffer silently from heartburn.)*
- ¼ could be Extroverts who prefer white food. *(For example, the Pillsbury Doughboy.)*
- ¼ could like both Spicy and white foods. *(If this isn't watched, the Baby could be way overweight. See photo of Baby in Chapter 11 watching his Grandpa take a Snooze.)*

Of course, it's probable, depending upon the side you sleep on, that ¼ could also be Extroverts who go for Spicy Foods.

No more needs to be said!

Then, too, if you are one of those who has a BIG Family, of the resulting offspring:

ITALIAN

	T	E	C
t	Tt	Et	Ct
e	Te	Ee	Ce
c	Tc	Ec	Cc

NORWEGIAN

- ⅑ could be Touchy, not touchy. *(Indifferent isn't so bad, though.)*
- ⅑ could be Extroverts who aren't touchy. *(Town Folks call these People aloof. Farmers say that these People think they are really something, then.)*
- ⅑ could be Catholics who aren't touchy. *(If you have to be a Catholic, this is probably the best way to go. These People make good nuns.)*

- ⅑ might be Touchy introverts. *(Many of these kids have a tough time in Junior High School and at Bible Camp.)*
- ⅑ would be Extrovert-introverts. *(Moody!)*
- ⅑ would be introverted Catholics. *(Low Church.)*
- ⅑ could be Touchy lutherans. *(These are responsible for Synod Mergers and are the kind that like to turn around in Church, shake hands with total strangers and give The Sign of Peace.)*
- ⅑ might be Extroverted lutherans. *(Good kind to pick for Sunday School Superintendents, but keep them off New Hymnal Committees.)*
- ⅑ could be Catholic-lutherans. *(Eventually, these People Turn becoming Episcopalians or Presbyterians. They aren't so choosy about who they step out with.)*

AN EXTROVERTED lutheran

Keep this type off the
New Hymnal Committees

Some of these mixed up cases were born following The War. More cases came about a few years after Country Schools closed and consolidated with Town Schools in the early '50s.

Two Morals or Lessons to be Learned From All This:	1. Remember where you came from. 2. Mating is Serious Stuff!

Assignment:

If you are Serious about mating and reproducing, or if you are supposed to Lead the Confirmands through the section on Falling in Love for Life, draw a few examples on your own!

ETHNIC or RELIGIOUS GROUP A

(_____)

ETHNIC or RELIGIOUS GROUP B

(_____)

NATIONALITY A

(_____)

NATIONALITY B

(_____)

We'd like to give credit to our daughters, Katrina Elise and Siri Elise, for teaching us what kids are learning in School these Days.

Kinds
of
Peas

Including Foreign Ones

3

KINDS OF PEAS, INCLUDING FOREIGN ONES

Just like Lutherans, there are many kinds of Peas. Both evolve, mutate, dry up and shrivel. Both are Down-to-Earth and sometimes get soaked. *(See Chapter 2 on **Mendel, Mixed Marriages and Recessive Genes.**)* Here is a list of some Peas and their particulars:

Main Croppers

Top Pod: 8 to 10 Peas per Pod
69 days growing time

These plump, bright Pea Pods are clustered near the top in a bunch. Because they open easily, they are good for the harried Housewife who has a lot of Chores, Field Work, and other Things to get done in a double quick hurry.

Wando: 7 to 9 Peas per Pod
70 days growing time

In order to have these ready by Decoration Day, you need an early Spring thaw. These have a good green color.

Novella: People who should know aren't sure how many Peas per Pod, so these are for Families where it doesn't matter.

64 to 65 days growing time depending upon the seed catalog.

When you plant two rows 8 to 10 inches apart, the tendrils—unlike Lutherans—will hold hands to support each other. Because these Peas are nearly leafless, they are good for Gardeners whose eyes are getting Creamy and dim, or for color-blind men.

Little Marvel: 7 to 8 Peas per Pod
62 days growing time

These spacesavers are good for City Folks who have Penny-Postcard-sized plots and no Farm Relatives.

Maestro: 9 to 11 Peas per Pod
61 days growing time

The seed catalog says you can grow these in the Fall, too, but People in the Dakotas know it could freeze before the first Home football game. Besides, their tastebuds are tuned into having Peas for Decoration Day and Squash on Labor Day, so Maestro seems appropriate only for People who live down South and do Things differently.

Laxton's Progress No. 9:

7 to 9 Peas per Pod
65 days growing time

These mush good for Babies and Older Folks without both Upper and Lower Plates.

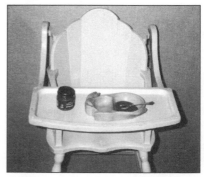

Green Arrow: 68 days growing time

These No-Nonsense, straight-as-an-arrow Peas average 11 Peas per Pod. You can't beat that, then!

Extra Early Croppers

Extra Early Alaska: 6 to 8 Peas per Pod
                           52 days growing time

A favorite of commercial Canners and People who like to enter Peas in the County Fair because the Peas are wrinkle-free so it isn't so tough to fool the judges. Almost guaranteed a Blue Ribbon, and if you're lucky, maybe a Purple Grand Champion.

Extra Early Little Marvel: 6 to 7 Peas per Pod
                                  63 days growing time

These dark green Decoration Day Peas shouldn't be confused with Plain Little Marvel Peas. Town women who have Deep Freezes like these for freezing.

Early Frosty: 6 to 7 Peas per Pod
                     63 days

Similar to Extra Early Little Marvels, but different. Usually a Double-Podder.

Edible Snap Pea Pods
for City and Uppity Folk

(Today Uppity Folks are called Yuppies.)

Sugar Daddy: 62 to 72 days growing time. Guess it doesn't much matter. You'll just have to be patient and see. These are for People who eat out a lot and don't like to gag in

public. They aren't so easy to Shell so they aren't the best for Farm women who Can. Farm men have never heard of People eating Pea Pods; they just feed them to the Pigs.

City Peas on a Doily

Sugar Snap: 68 days growing time Versatile and Practical as far as City Things go because you can eat the Pod and all, or Shell them like Normal Peas and Normal People do.

Sugar Ann: 56 days growing time
She's just like the Sugar Snap, but she's not a turtle. She struts her Stuff two weeks before the Sugar Snap.

Foreign Peas

Oregon Sugar Pod II: 60 days growing time
The young Pods are brittle and stringless and good for stir-fry
Oriental Recipes. These are also eaten by semi-retired Ministers and their Families who have been Missionaries in China.

Black-eyed Peas: This must be Southern Stuff.

Cow Peas: You won't find any of these maroon-eyed purple-hulled Peas in any Lutheran Church Cookbooks, just in the seed catalogs.

Canadian Peas: Field Peas with small seeds and pinkish Flowers that are grown for 4–H in Canada and a few places in the Northern States.

Swedish Peas: Sometimes known as Pea Soup Peas or yellow Peas.

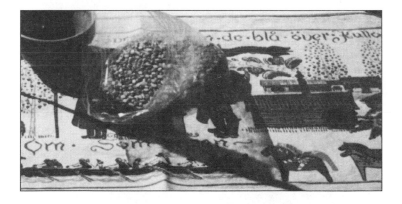

Peas That Aren't for Eating

Sweet Peas: Used for Fancyin' Up Tables and yards or for Depression-era bridal bouquets.

Caragana Peas: Hedge-growing, yellow-blossom Peas that are good for Serving Cousins and dolls at the Playhouse in the Woods. *(See Chapter 17.)*

The Art of Eating
Cream Peas on Toast

4

THE ART OF EATING
CREAM PEAS ON TOAST

The following Directions for eating Cream Peas on Toast are for right-handed men.* *(Women should eat Cream Peas on Toast by sitting up straight, and, before starting to eat, use both the Knife and Fork to cut up half a piece of Toast at one time into Ladies Aid–sized bites.)*

Commence with these Directions as soon as Grace has been said and the Plate of Toast has been passed:

1. With your elbows firmly planted on the Table, and your left arm *(see photo)* curled around the edge of the Plate with fingers touching the North–Northeast end of the Plate, lean forward in your Chair and begin.

---

* Left-handed men need only put her in reverse, sit at the opposite side of the Table or turn the Book upside-down.

2. Starting at the Southwest corner, cut a generous piece with your Fork.

3. Spear the piece of Toast like you would spear a Haybale with a Pitchfork, making sure the Toast gets well-soaked.

4. Shove this in your mouth.

5. Continue in a Northeast Direction until you're down to the last two pieces.

6. Pierce the remaining two pieces together, one on top of the other, and with a circular counter-clockwise motion, mop up any Peas and Cream remaining on the Plate.

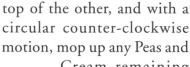

7. Wipe your face with a convenient Norwegian-Lutheran Farm Napkin.

(In a pinch, this Practical and Useful Napkin can double as a Hanky in the Field.)

8. When you finish, push your Plate to the center of the Table, lean back and fold your hands over your stomach and wait for The Mrs. to bring Coffee.

(If you're in a hurry to go do Chores, drink from the Saucer.)

The Art of Eating Cooked Peas
Traill County–Style*

These Directions are for right-handed men. **

For the Traill County Pea–eating Method, a right-handed man holds the Knife in his right hand and the Fork in his left hand. *(Unless you have had too much* devil's drink *that makes you do foolish Things, make sure the cutting edge of the Knife faces the center of the Table, not you.)*

To make sure you get this right, pretend your Plate is the North 40. Your Fork is then perpendicular to the West boundary, and your Knife is perpendicular to the East edge. The sharp edge of the Knife is then facing the North boundary. Another advantage of this Knife placement is that the

---

* Traill County Style Pea–eating spread throughout the Midwest via traveling Hired Help.

** Left-handed men need only put her in reverse, sit at the opposite side of the Table or turn the book upside-down. (Women only did this when they ate alone, like when the kids were in bed and The Husband was still out Shockin' Oats.)

sharp edge is then facing the Direction that the Peas will be herded from by the Fork. *(You, of course, are then sitting South of the North 40.)*

Steady hands and a flat Plate are required to use the Traill County Method. With the Knife in your right hand and the Fork in your left, herd the Peas with the Fork onto the Knife blade. Leaning forward and bending down to minimize spillage, have the Knife meet your mouth. Repeat until the Peas are gone.

The most accomplished Traill County Pea–eaters never dropped a Pea during the entire Meal, even when they had more than one row lined up on the blade.

The Art of Eating Peas Kid-Style

The way I like green Peas the most,
Is not on Spuds and not on Toast.

Eating Peas just like a kid,
Is not from a Jar with a gray zinc lid.

You bend way down in your Garden plot,
And shove 'em in till you've had a lot.

Wipe 'em off and Shuck the ends,
If you eat the Shells, you'll get the bends.

Baby Cream Peas

Peas in a Pod

A Photo Essay

Two Trees and a Runt

5

PEAS IN A POD
A Photo Essay

Norwegian-Lutherans are more at Peace with themselves when Things are alike. They never went much for social mixers or much into mixing Things. They were just more Comfortable when everything stayed the same and nothing stood out. "Just like Peas in a Pod" was a Common phrase used among Norwegian-Lutheran Farmers to describe Things that were Normal. Here are some examples of Normal Things.

**Two Peas
in a Pod**

**No-Nonsense Stockings
and Sensible Shoes**

Twins Who Read for the Minister

North Dakota
Twins Posing
by King Olav
the V's Car at
the Høstfest

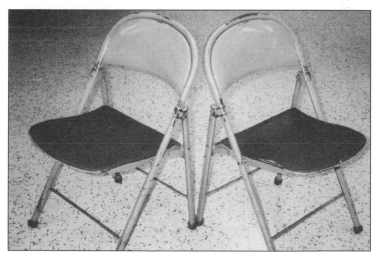

Padded Lutheran Church Basement Chairs

Three Peas in a Pod

Triune Lutheran Doors in Wisconsin

Three Norwegian-American Wood Carvers

Three Easter Bonnets with "See-Thru"
Nylon Dresses on Three Lutheran Sisters
(NOTE: THE OLDER ONE GOT TO WEAR NYLON STOCKINGS)

Cinch-Waist Circle Skirts from the Cities
(NOTE: NORWEGIAN-LUTHERAN FARM BROOM
HANGING OUTSIDE)

Four Peas in a Pod

Four Towheads Who Eat Cream Peas on Christmas

Five Peas in a Pod

Five Johnson Farm Boys in a Row

(AS YOU CAN SEE, THREE HAD ALREADY BEEN CONFIRMED)

Six Peas in a Pod

Six Company Jello-Os

Seven Peas in a Pod

Ladies Aid at O.T. Rovang Farm: Mrs. Finsand, Mrs. Espeseth, Petra
Berge, Mrs. Martha Bye, Mrs. Pete Gulbranson and Mrs. Rovang
Seven Country Ladies Aid Ladies
OUT OF THE KITCHEN, BUT STILL IN THE HEAT

Eight
Peas
in a
Pod

Eight City Ladies Aid Ladies

**Eight Johnson Hallings
Who Should Have Been Svensons**

**Nine
Peas
in a
Pod**

**Nine Linoleum Squares in
Church Basement Green**

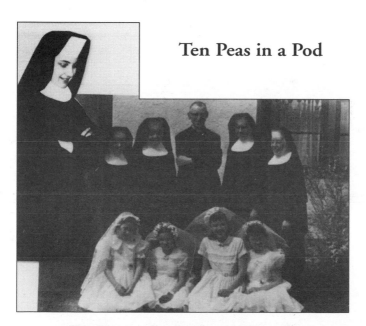

Ten Peas in a Pod

Ten Norwegian-Lutheran Wannabes

Puttin' Up

6

PUTTIN' UP

In Norwegian-American, Puttin' Up is what the Swedish- and Danish-Americans call Canning and what the Town People called Preserving. It is hard Work, but when Winter comes you'll be Thankful you Put Up with it.

Being Thankful in the Winter

Gettin' Ready to Put Up Peas

1. Get up before the Chickens.
2. Put on an Old Housedress, a sturdy Ever-Day* Apron, and your Garden Wedgies.
3. Get the big White Enamel Bowl.
4. Go to the Garden. Bend over and start pickin'.
5. Place Peas in Washbowl *(see photo below)*.

6. When the Bowl is full, empty it in a container on the Picnic Table and pick another Bowl full.
7. Pick about 16 gallons for an average-sized Canning.
8. Sit at the Picnic Table and start Shellin' (Shuckin' **).
9. Get the kids to help Shell/Shuck so you have enough for Noon Dinner *(see last photo)*.

---

* The correct spelling is "everyday," but for Norwegian-Lutheran Folk the "y" was silent just like the "-*ed* " in Cream*ed* Peas.

** Depending on whether your Family came from the East or the West side of the Dovrefjell in Norway, you will call removing the outer casing of the Peas Shuckin' or Shellin' respectively.

10. To Shuck properly, run your fingernail along the inside Seam of the Pod.

11. Strip the Pod into a Bowl by running your thumb down the inside.*

12. After about four hours of Pea-Shellin', or when you have about enough to fill the White Enamel Bowl and then some *(see last photo again)*, you're ready to start Puttin' Up.

13. Have the kids feed the Shells/Shucks to the Pigs.

Some girls are just like Peas...
They lose their freshness as
soon as they are picked!

---

* Etiquette Clue: If you Shuck/Shell on Saturday, you'll want to wear White Gloves to Church on Sunday because there's no way you'll get the green stain out from under your thumbnail until after Wash Day on Monday.

Directions for Puttin' Up Peas

There are three ways to Put Up, but only two really count: Hot-Water Bath Canning and the New-Fangled Pressure Cooker Method. *(Freezing was used by those who were lazy or otherwise occupied.)*

The Pressure Cooker Method was mainly used by Town women, the young Seminarian's Wife, and by Farm women who weren't afraid to experiment.

Hot-Water Bath Canning was the preferred Method used by Norwegian-American-Lutheran Farm women because:

- it was the least expensive way of Puttin' Up,
- the water could be re-used for different purposes, and
- it didn't require anything Fancy.

Hot-Water Bath Canning:

Put washed Peas in washed Jars leaving half an inch empty at the top.

Pour in boiling water to fill up the Jar.

Put on the sterilized lids and screw rings.

Lower the Jars into a Kettle of boiling water, boiling for 3½ hours.

Take out and listen for the Jars to Seal.

Pressure Cooker Method:

Peas have to be Pressure-Cookered for maybe about 40 minutes.

Follow the Directions that came with your Pressure Cooker.

Jar of Peas
Put Up by Genevieve Dodge
of Minneapolis in 1934!!!

Sunday Supper

Cream Peas Recipes

7

SUNDAY SUPPER
Cream Peas Recipes

There is a Simple reason why Cream Peas on Toast was a favorite: It was a Simple, Plain Meal. No spices, no Butter, no Fuss. Served with a Side of Spam and a Bowl of Rhubarb Sauce, it was a perfect Meal. Cream Peas on Toast was the ultimate Comfort Food.

A Perfect Complement

Cream Peas on Toast was often Served on Sunday Nights for Supper in Lutheran Households because it was a way of providing a Hot Meal without heating up the Kitchen. It didn't require a lot of Fussin' and Stewin', what with it being a Day of Rest and all that.

However, Holy Roman Catholics in the Upper Midwest often had Cream Peas on Toast on Friday Nights when they couldn't have meat. Otherwise, the reasons for making Catholic Cream Peas were the same as for Lutherans, except Friday wasn't a Day of Rest. Of course, Good Friday was kind of an exception except that it was okay to Plant Potatoes and Peas in the Garden that Day.

One Thing that maybe made Cream Peas on Toast Special was that it was always Served on Town (Bought*en*) Bread. There was a Practical reason for this, too. Homemade Bread didn't fit so well in the Flip-Down-the-Sides Toasters. *(See cover photo.)* Topped off with a Dish of Sauce for Dessert, this Meal was as close to Heaven as most thought they could get here on Earth.

Even though everyone who was interviewed *(see Chapter 18)* said they really liked Cream Peas on Toast, it wasn't so easy to find a Recipe for it because no one wrote it down. Just like running Chokecherries through Cheesecloth, making Cream Peas on Toast was like slipping into your second skin. Women just knew how to do it. Variations came about because People used what they had on hand.

There are two winners and two runners-up in the Upper Midwest Contest for Cream Peas on Toast Recipes. These women won for two reasons:

• They wrote down the Recipe

• Folks said it was the best and that's good enough, then.

The Winner!

Fløtet Erter
På Brød

Melt 4 T. Butter in a Pan. Stir in 2 level T. of Flour. Then add 1 c. whole Milk and bring to a boil. Add the cooked Peas. Salt and pepper to taste. If it is too thick, Simply add more Milk. Serve over Toast made with Town or Bought*en* Bread.

SUBMITTED BY CATHARINE WENSTROM

Second Place

Cream Peas on Toast

Melt about 3 or 4 T. Butter in Kettle. Add about 3 to 4 T. Flour. Stir well but do not burn. Add about 2 c. Milk or more. Cook until thick. Add Peas. Salt and pepper it. Serve over Toast made with Town (Bough*ten)* Bread.

SUBMITTED BY MRS. MERRILL (IRENE) MORTENSEN

Runners-Up

Cream Peas on Toast

2 c. Peas	4 T. Flour
2 T. Butter	2 c. Milk

¼ t. pepper

Melt Butter and blend in Flour, then Milk and pepper. Cook until thick. Stir to prevent lumping. Mix in the Peas and cook five minutes more. This can be Served on either Toast or Mashed Potatoes.

SUBMITTED BY MRS. SANBORN OLSON

Cream*ed* Leftovers

Left-over meat can be Creamed with Peas and Served in Toast Cups made in Cupcake tins.

SUBMITTED BY MRS. GEORGE JENSON

How to Stretch It

There is also an unwritten Recipe called Cream Peas for a Crowd or How to Stretch It. Basically, you just don't drain the liquid from the Peas. People have heard about it, but no one knows anyone who has tried it.

SUBMITTED BY *Anonymous*

After the Parade on Decoration Day

Other Things That Are Cream(ed)

8

OTHER THINGS
THAT ARE CREAM*(ed)*

DRY BEEF
Referred to as Dried Beef in Town and as Chipped Beef
in the Army.

PLAIN CREAM on BREAD
Served with Karo Syrup or Homemade Chokecherry Jelly.

TUNA
Preferred by Farm Folks.

SALMON
Preferred by Town Folks.

CARROTS

CORN

CHEESE

Cream Cheese is mainly used by Town People and Today's
Yuppies. *(Farmers prefer Cottage Cheese.)*

PRIMOST

No explanation needed.

COFFEE

Especially used by Swedish-Lutherans
or for Silver Weddings.

BUTTER and SUGAR

Cream can be a verb, too. Creaming Butter and Sugar
sounds more Sensible than mixing. Norwegian-Lutherans
don't go in much for mixing.

PUFF

Cream puffs can be Yuppie Food, a name for a kitten,
or a reference to a cheerleader.

of TARTAR

Some sort of spice, but just pepper and Salt
are all one really needs. Some say it helps make meringue
higher on lemon pie. If you think you have money to
throw around, try it. *(It's White.)*

SAUCE on LUTEFISK

Melted Butter is just fine, too.

COLOR

Cream-colored Kitchen walls are nice because
they match the Food and the Ivy will stand out nicely,
but it's not too Practical if you have small kids.

FOOTBALL PLAYERS

Usually with nine-man teams.

Cream of the Crop

THIS IS MOST CERTAINLY TRUE!

Lutheran
Hotdish Recipes
with
Peas in Them

9

LUTHERAN HOTDISH RECIPES WITH PEAS IN THEM

Glorified Hash

Leftover meat, Potatoes, Peas, Onion

1 c. Bread or Cracker Crumbs
2 Eggs

Leftover gravy or Milk
2 tsp. catsup

Mix these together and mold into balls or patties. Pan fry or Bake in a Moderate Oven for 45 minutes.

Russian Fluff

1 ½ lb. hamburger
1 No. 2 can tomatoes
1 c. mushrooms, not drained

1 c. cooked Rice
1 c. Peas
Half a green pepper

1 diced Onion, any size

Combine fried hamburger, boiled Rice, Peas, undrained mushrooms, pepper and Onion.

Put in Buttered Baking Dish and sprinkle top with Buttered Bread Crumbs.

Bake 45 minutes at 375 degrees.

If you need more, add more hamburger and Rice.

Spam Hotdish

1 can Spam, cubed	1 stalk celery, chopped
1 sm. can Peas	1 can cheap mushroom Soup
1 sm. Onion, chopped	1 green pepper, chopped
1 can chow mein noodles	Pepper; NO Salt

Cook celery; brown Spam, Onion and green pepper. Grease Hotdish Bowl.

Combine Peas, celery, Spam, Onion and green pepper. Alternate this with layers of noodles and mushroom Soup that has been thinned with liquid from can of Peas.

Bake at 350 degrees until it's done.

**Picnic Lunch Break after Looking at the Fields
on Sunday Afternoon**

Hotdish with Eggs

2 c. boiled Spuds, cubed
1 c. Peas
1 T. cut pimiento

5 hard-cooked Eggs, cut
1 T. fine-sliced Onion
Salt and pepper to taste

2 c. White Sauce *(or more, if you like)*

Place in Buttered Hotdish Bowl and top with grated Cheese. Bake 20 minutes at 350 degrees.

You can also add celery and maybe other Things, if you want.

Dry Beef Hotdish

¼ or ⅓ lb. smoked dry beef
1 can water poured over dry beef
1 c. cut up Cheese
1 sm. can Peas

1 can mushroom Soup
1 c. cut up celery
1 sm. chopped Onion
½ lb. medium noodles,
    broken up

Mix all together and put in Baking Dish.
Bake 1½ hours at 350 degrees.

Vegetable Hotdish

6 med. Onions
2 c. cooked diced carrots
2 c. cooked Peas

¼ c. Buttered Bread Crumbs
½ tsp. Salt
¼ tsp. pepper

¼ c. grated American Cheese

Boil Onions in Saltwater until tender and drain. Add carrots and Peas. Pour enough Cream Sauce over vegetables to cover. Sprinkle top with Cheese and Bread Crumbs and Bake at 400. Serve very Hot.

Potato Chips and Tuna Hotdish

½ lb. Potato chips
1 can tuna
1 sm. can Peas

1 can on-sale mushroom Soup
1 c. Hot Milk

Alternate layers of chips, tuna, and Peas in a greased Baking Dish. Add Milk to the Soup and pour over ingredients in Baking Dish. Bake at 350 degrees.

Hot Hamburger Hotdish

1 ½ lb. hamburger
2 T. Fat
1 Onion
2 c. Garden Peas
2 c. raw diced carrots

2 c. raw diced Spuds
1 c. diced celery
1 can tomato Soup *(whatever is on sale)*
½ tsp. Salt & ⅛ tsp. pepper

Brown the meat and Onion in the Fat. Add tomato Soup, vegetables, Salt and pepper. Bake in Buttered Baking Dish at 350 for 45 minutes.

Chicken Hotdish #1

1 Chicken
1 pkg. ring Macaroni
1 can Peas

2 c. Milk
2 T. Butter
3 hard-boiled Eggs

1 can mushroom or similar Soup

Boil Chicken until well done. Remove meat from Bones and dice. Cook Macaroni rings. Grease Baking Dish and put Macaroni, Peas, diced Chicken and Soup in layers.

Make a White Sauce with the Butter, Flour and Milk and pour over. Top with Bread Crumbs or Shredded Wheat. Bake at 350 for 40 minutes.

Chicken Hotdish #2

2 c. cooked Chicken
1 c. Cream
3 c. Cracker or other Crumbs

Chicken broth
½ can Peas
Pepper & Salt to taste

(You can add grated Onion, if you want)

Layer Chicken, then Peas, then Crumbs until Baking Dish is full. Pour Cream and broth over top to cover layers. Top with Crumbs.

Bake in Moderate Oven about 40 minutes.

Grandma Carlson's Chicken Hotdish

1 big Chicken
1 c. diced carrots
1 c. diced Potatoes

1 can Peas
1 sm. Onion
1 c. diced celery

Salt and pepper to taste

Cook Chicken until done; Bone and dice it.

Use broth to make gravy.

Put all in layers in Hotdish Bowl with a sprinkle of Flour between layers. Add broth last and a little Cream and Bake.

This is an Old Recipe so you can make changes and substitute other things.

Occasions When Cream Peas Just Won't Do

You Just Don't Serve Cream Peas on Toast
at Bible Camp

10

OCCASIONS WHEN CREAM PEAS JUST WON'T DO

Substitute Recipes

There are some Occasions when Cream Peas on Toast just won't do. Most of these are Occasions that involve more than the Family—Things like Farmers' Union Potlucks, Sunday School Picnics, *Bygdelag* Reunions, Family Reunions, Norway Day and Silver Weddings or Picnics away from Home.

Here are some good, Practical, Lutheran Farm Recipes

Confirmation Peas

Substitute: Lime Jell-O Salad

Make lime or lemon Jell-O.

Add grated carrots and thawed, frozen Peas.

Set it in a ring mold.

If you are expecting a Crowd, double the Recipe and set in a Cakepan.

Serve on lettuce with mayo topping. *(Optional)*

to substitute on these Occasions.

Sunday School Picnic Peas
and/or Potluck Peas for Doings
at Farmers' Union, Farm Bureau, the Grange, or other
Big Events where Bulk is Required

Substitute: 'Tater Tot Hotdish
(Warning: This Recipe calls for Store-bought products.)

1 lb. ground beef *(seasoned, depending on the age group
   that you're Serving)*
1 pkg. frozen mixed vegetables *(can substitute 1 small can
   Peas, drained)*
1 can Cream Chicken Soup *(whatever brand is on sale)*
½ can water
½ pack cheap Onion Soup mix
Bag of 'tater tots

Put frozen 'tater tots on top. Arrange them pretty if you're
up to it.

Put in 425 degree Oven for one hour and then turn down
to 375 degrees for ½ hour more or thereabouts.

Wedding Peas
and/or Ladies Aid Peas *

Substitute: Cold Chicken or Tuna Salad

2 c. cold boiled Chicken *(or can of drained tuna)*

some cubed celery   6 hard-boiled Eggs
mayo to moisten   small Jar chopped pimiento

seasoning *(depending on the age group)*
Add enough Peas to look pretty.

Mix it all together.

Just before Serving, moisten with mayo.

Depending on the group, Serve it on lettuce or with cold-water Buns.

Sprinkle with paprika, if you have it. Don't go buy it just for this because you'll never use it all up and then it would go to waste.

(* Eventually, after several Mergers and fights about the Communist-inspired Red Hymnal, these became known as Circle Peas.)

4-H or Luther League Peas

Just remember to make a lot.
You don't want to run out!

Mother–Daughter Banquets

Substitute: Spring Medley

1 c. celery cut up	1½ c. med. White Sauce
1 ½ c. fresh Peas	¾ c. Rice
6 to 8 sm. carrots	¼ lb. nippy Cheese, grated
1 sm. head cauliflower	Parsley

Cook vegetables separately in boiling Saltwater. Drain and combine with White Sauce.

Cook Rice in boiling Saltwater; drain and pat on bottom and sides of greased Baking Dish. Cover with Cheese and heat in Moderate Oven until delicately browned.

Pour Cream vegetables into Rice mold. Garnish with parsley. Serve right away.

Yuppie and/or City Peas

Substitute: Snow Pea Salad

(Normally you won't have these ingredients on hand. If you want to try it, you'll have to make an extra trip to Town so this can get pretty expensive.)

¼ c. red wine vinegar	1 c. Cream
¼ c. oil	6 artichoke hearts *(Canned or frozen)*
2 tsp. Dijon mustard	2 c. thinly sliced fresh mushrooms
1 tsp. crushed garlic	1½ c. fresh Snow Peas, trimmed
1 tsp. dried dill weed	& halved

½ c. sliced toasted almonds

Combine vinegar, oil, mustard, garlic, dill weed, and Salt & pepper to taste. Pour Cream into mixture in a slow stream and whisk it to blend.

Toss vegetables with dressing and garnish with almonds.

Pea Soup

The Swedish Contribution

11

PEA SOUP

The Swedish Contribution

One Sunday Afternoon right after Dinner, Gustavus Adolphus, his brother, brother-in-law and the Hired Man, Hjalmer, decided to go look at the Fishfields that Gustaf, as his Friends called him, had in the North Sea.

He was anxious to see if the Fish he had thrown in during Spring Planting had grown any bigger. It had been two weeks since he had checked on his Fishbeds because the Sunday before, his oldest son, Gustavus Adolphus the III, the one who would inherit the Family Fishfarm, was Confirmed.*

According to everyone at Augustana Lutheran Church that Morning, it looked like it was going to be a nice Day. But sometimes, as Gustaf knew from past experience, the Weather—like a woman—could change face faster than you could say *Hälsa Dem Därhemma*. Sure as shootin', that's what happened.

When they were 14 miles out to Sea but still six miles North of Karl Johan Karlsson's Fishbed, a beastly Easterly Wind blew up out of nowhere taking them through the Danish *Skagerrak* and out to Sea. After several Days, and to

---

* He did really good at Catechization, and his voice had already changed.

make a long story short, they ended up on Shore in a strange place that was shaped like a Dakota or Wyoming Cowboy Boot.

Since they didn't have a Lunch Pail on board or even a Thermos of Coffee, they walked into Town for Supper. There was no Sense to what they saw. Grown men were walking down the street greeting everyone—men and women alike— with hugs and touching. Gustaf felt uneasy, put his head down and disgustedly shook his head at these loud, boisterous Lost Souls he met. He thought to himself: They're just the caliber of Folks who would clap right out loud in Church, too, and think nothing of it.

They walked into what looked like a *Kaffestuga.*

Since they didn't understand the language they just pointed to the chalkboard hoping they would get some-

thing Sensible like a Hot beef Sandwich with Mashed Potatoes or, as Hjalmer the Hired Help said, "I sure could go for some Cream Peas on Toast." But as luck would have it, they didn't get anything Decent.

The short, plump lady with bright, dangly red earrings, somewhat of a mustache, and dark hair pulled back in a Bun, set down in front of them what looked for all the world like a Bowl full of long, White angle worms—good for Fishing but not much for eating unless, of course, you were a Walleye(d) Pike, Northern or Cod.

The Food was so spicy that, in spite of all the starving kids in China, they couldn't even lick the Platter Clean and so they just said, "*Uff da. Neimen,* What in the World Next!" and left to go back to the Boat.

On their way back, Gustaf got a bad case of heartburn from all the spice, and they decided to take a Snooze under a Tree looking for all the world like four Peas in a Pod.

Taking a Snooze #1
(This is how they laid, then.)

When they woke up they thought they were having a bad dream. Barefoot women with baskets on their heads

Taking a Snooze #2

were singing, dancing and carrying on like all get-out while they were squishin' and stompin' with their feet what looked to be large, green, Early June Peas. *(Of course, we know now that, in actuality, it was green grapes that were being prepared for the* devil's drink.*)*

Gustaf said, "I think it's time we head back Home where Things are Normal." Gustaf had a good Sense of Direction and in no time flat they were back Home in Sweden.

After Chores, while eating Lunch after Supper that Night, Gustaf told His Wife, Serena, about the Foreign heathens he had seen singing and squishin' and stompin' what looked like all the world to be big Early June Peas.

As she was dunking her *Pepperkaker,* Serena-Beata *— being the clever Housewife she was—thought to herself: Maybe this is a new Recipe I could put in the Augustana Lutheran's 200th Anniversary Heritage Cookbook, then. But since she was too Modest and Sensible to dance and smash Peas with her bare feet, she just smashed the Peas with her Potato Masher, cooked them up and the rest is history.

---

* She was named after her Grandmas on both sides.

Swedes all over are known for their famous Pea Soup—either green split from the Italian grape connection, or yellow split to match the Swedish Flag which makes a good centerpiece.

Swedish Pea Soup

1 ham Bone	1 Onion, cut up
3 qts. water	1½ c. celery

1 pkg. whole or split yellow or green Peas

Peas must be soaked overnight.
Drain and put all ingredients in a Soup Kettle.
Bring to a boil and cook at least two hours on low heat.

Martin Luther

The German Affiliation
with Catholic Overtones
and an Augsburg Association (AA)

12

MARTIN LUTHER

The German Affiliation
with Catholic Overtones
and an Augsburg Association (AA)

Peas and Peace

One Night Martin Luther was lying in bed but he had had so much Coffee he couldn't get to sleep. He got to thinking about the Pope and he thought: I wonder why he thinks he's so good? He isn't even German! Luther Tossed and Turned and Fretted and Stewed and thought it was about time someone gave the Pope a run for his money. It was about time that someone stood up to him and all his High Falutin' Fanciness, frilly collars, Fish on Friday and other foolishness.

Martin, always being good with a quill, figured he'd list his gripes so he started right away in the Morning and worked straight through until late Saturday Afternoon when he had to take his bath so he could go to Town that Night. After visiting with his Neighbors in Town and shootin' the bull for a while, Luther decided the time was ripe. Tonight was as good as any time.

After the Respectable People had Gone Home, just after the 9:00 Drawing, Luther went over to the All Saints' Holy Roman Catholic Church and pounded his 95 Theses on the door. He had really hit the nail on the head, but he was hoping all the commotion wouldn't wake up the Holy Roman Emperor who slept in the Church and bowed to the Pope and kissed his feet.

The next Morning when everyone showed up in Church for the 10 o'clock Service, the Holy Roman Emperor, who was clearly hoppin' mad, stood up in front of the Church and asked "Who put this on the door, then?" as he held up the 95 Theses. Martin, who normally kept to himself, couldn't Put Up with it any longer. He stood up and said, "Here I Stand. I can do no other, then." The Emperor got spittin' mad and couldn't pay attention to the rest of the Service.

The Emperor thought he would fix Martin so he banned him from coming to Church. Martin thought he would get even so on the last Sunday in October—eventually named Reformation Day—he went to the Church and hid behind the Caragana Hedge *(see Chapter 17 on Playhouse Peas)* and thought: What a Mighty Fortress! He then began to shoot Peas through his Pea Shooter right at the front of the Church. When the Holy Roman Emperor came down the front steps, he slipped on the Peas and fell flat on his backend, splitting his pants. Martin figured he had really Creamed the guy, but he had done so much more. He had Canned him too. The Emperor's fall really symbolized the permanent split between the Catholics and the Lutherans. Things would never be the same. He had split his pants and the Church once and for all.

This sentiment was reflected in the famous words of Charles the V, the Holy Roman Catholic Emperor in 1521, who boldly stated to Luther and to anyone else who was interested, "Unless I am refuted and convicted by testimonies of the Scriptures or by clear arguments...my conscience is bound in the Word of God. I cannot and will not recant anything, Peas included." *(The Old German script for this is somewhat smudged, but it most likely says this or something like it.)*

This revealed a firmness and setness that has been Passed Down to this Generation. To this Day, German-Lutheran Farms kids are taught: You made your bed, now lie in it!

This split, of course, opened up many possibilities for Luther. He took off for Augsburg where he figured Things would be more liberal and where he, too, could get an Education for Society.

Norwegian-Lutherans in America continue this Tradition even Today enrolling and buying sweatshirts at Augsburg College in Minneapolis, which is located smack-dab in the middle of heathens, Christians, hippies, heretics and just about anything you can think of and surrounding Murphy Square. To this Day, Augsburg College continues to send Well-Meaning Do-Gooders out into society.

Well-Meaning Do-Gooders
Sent into Society

The Moral of this story is: Never Under-estimate the Strength of the Reformation, The Persistence of the Lutheran Tradition, or the Power of Peas.

(Epilogue: Soon thereafter, the Town of Wittenberg did away with Saturday Night Drawings because they just seemed to pit one Farmer against the other and then, too, some said that the usual prize, Pope on a Rope Soap, could be seen as heresy.)

The Princess and the Pea
on the Prairie

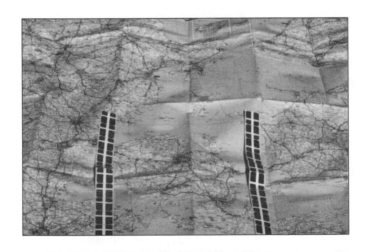

The Danish Tie

13

THE PRINCESS AND THE PEA ON THE PRAIRIE

The Danish Tie

I

This story is a variation on Hans Christian Andersen's story, The Princess on the Pea. In case you don't remember it, there once was a Prince who wanted to marry a Princess but he wanted The Real McCoy, no Floozies and no Fakes, so he travelled to Beat the Band but something always went wrong. It just wasn't Workin' Out for him so he got down and out and came Home.

One Evening a terrible Corker blew up from the West. Then there was a knock at the Town gate. It was a Princess, all right, but she looked a Fright because of the Weather. The Rain ran down her whole body—through the holes in her Beaded Hair Net, down the sleeves of her Shorty Coat, down to the hem of her Gathered Circle Skirt, down her legs— into the heels of her Wedgies and out the open toes. She looked like a Rainspout. The Queen *(she was a clever one)* said, "I'm going to figure this one out. Is she The Real Thing or not? Let's see if she puts her money where her mouth is."

First the Queen put an Extra Early Little Marvel Pea on the green and White Linoleum floor *(see photo in Chapter 5)*.

Then she took 20 mattresses and laid them on top of the Pea and put 20 Homemade, Patchwork Mission Quilts on top of the mattresses. On top of this she put a rubber pee-sheet, just in case, and then covered it with a bottom sheet. She told the so-called Princess to "Sleep Tight and Don't Let the Bedbugs Bite." In the Morning, the Queen asked the so-called Princess, "How did it go, then?" The so-called Princess said, "It was such a lumpy bed that I'm black and blue all over." Now they knew she was The Real McCoy because through the 20 mattresses and 20 Patchwork Quilts, one rubber pee-sheet *(which hadn't been necessary)* and one bottom White starched cotton sheet, she had felt the Pea. No one but a real Princess could be so finicky!

So the Prince took her as His Mrs. for she was just the ticket he was looking for, and the Pea was put in a museum in Askov and it is there now unless some hoodlums broke in and took it. *(It is also part of a traveling exhibit and goes to Tyler each year for Aebleskiver Days.)*

This is Most Certainly True.

II

This next story is another variation on this same story. It happened to Hans Christian Andersen's grandson, Hans Luther Anderson, III, who had moved to the Dakota Prairie 100 years after the original story was written.

Once upon a time there was a Hog and Small Grain Farmer who Lived in the most Rural part of Dakota *(Southwest of Fargo, North Dakota; Northwest of Sioux Falls, South Dakota; and Due West of Herman, Minnesota—Home of many Lutheran Bachelor Farmers who like to be in the limelight)*. He needed a Wife, but he wasn't having much luck. It was like the women around there had been picked Clean as a Pea

Patch. The Locals that were left either made Hans Luther feel edgy or were too outgoing. One even commented how she liked his Pick-Up.

One Day he got up his Nerve and put an ad in the November edition of the DAKOTA FARMER in the Help Wanteds.

> **NEEDED:** One sturdy & hefty woman with a strong back. Must know how to Work hard and cook for Her Man without complaining. Needed by Spring Planting. Please send a Recipe. Swedes need not apply.

He ran a similar version of the ad in the DECORAH POSTEN. It said:

> *Kjære, Herre Gud,*
> *De som alting veit;*
> *Vil du skuffa meg ei kjerring,*
> *Som er både tjuk og feit!*
>
> *tr.* Dear, Lord God,
>   You who know everything;
>   Will you send me a woman
>   Who is both thick and fat.

Boy, oh boy, did Hans Luther get some foolish responses back.

One woman said she had seen a Picture of the Prairie Sunset and thought it would be Peas-ful. Another said she'd like to go see a rodeo. One said she had met a horse rustler at the Armour Meatpacking Plant in South St. Paul and thought if Hans Luther was anything like that guy, well, why not?

Hans threw out all the dreamers.

Another woman sent him a Recipe for Company 'Tater Tot Hotdish *(see Recipe below),* and the fifth woman sent a Recipe for Watermelon Pickles.

Hans threw out all the foolish ones.

A woman from Des Moines sent a Recipe for Chicken Hotdish, but it only called for half a can of Peas. Hans Luther wondered what she would do with the other half and what kind of a woman she must be if she bought Town Peas instead of Canning them herself.

Then there was the Recipe for Salmon Hotdish from another loose woman. Her Recipe called for a No. 2 can of Peas, a can of salmon and Breakfast Cereal.

Hans threw out the extravagant ones.

'Tater Tot Hotdish

(This Recipe only works if you have a Deep Freeze)

1 lb. ground beef
1 pkg. frozen mixed vegetables
1 can Cream*ed* Chicken Soup *(whatever brand is on sale)*
½ can water
½ pack cheap Onion Soup mix

Put frozen 'tater tots on top. Put in 425 degree Oven for one hour and then turn down to 375 degrees for a half hour more.

For Company, double or triple or quadruple everything depending on how many are coming. To Fancy it Up for Company, Serve with Company Jell-O *(see page 35 in* LUTHERAN CHURCH BASEMENT WOMEN).

In the end there were only two possibilities, and they both had sent in Recipes for Cream Peas on Toast. One of them had a post office box so just to be safe, Hans Luther chose the one with the RR address.

Her name was Hilda Hansen and she Lived for a long time on the Prairie.

This is Most Certainly True!

The End

The St. Olaf Connection

Fram, Fram,
Kristmenn, Krossmenn

14

THE ST. OLAF CONNECTION
Fram, Fram, Kristmenn, Krossmenn

In the liberal '60s and '70s Lutheran colleges across the nation had their hands full and their Chapels empty. Students were organizing petition Drives for legalized dancing* on campus and everything else that smacked of Moral Decay.

Kids were trying to find themselves and like Sven Ole Nestegaard said as boldly as he could to the President of St. Olaf College, "Now think about it. How can my boy get lost? He's only 150 miles from Home. Good Night, then! He was born with an innate Sense of NESW, and since he was three years old he knew the Loftgaard Place was three and a half miles Southeast of the North 40 that Grandpa bought in '57 when Ezra Taft Benson, that Mormon who didn't know anything about Parity with all their wives and everything, was Secretary of Agriculture."

All sorts of Things were happening in the world and Norwegian-Lutheran Farm kids felt it was High Time to go the whole nine yards and question a few Things. Things like: If dancing is a sin, why do Lutheran Parents approve of,

---

* Students at Concordia College shook up the Faithful alumni when they demanded to call a spade a spade and changed the name from "square gaming" to square dancing.

and enjoy, watching Lawrence Welk and all the Champagne Music Makers sing and dance while hard liquor bubbles are bursting all over the black and White Motorola? If working in the Fields on Sunday is a sin, why isn't working and cooking in the Kitchen a sin?

They questioned deep Things too: If Lutheran-Norwegian-Christians (both ALC-ers and ELC-ers) were not to judge anyone, why were some Norwegians buried outside the perimeters of the Norwegian-Lutheran Cemetery? Was that an example of *Fram, Fram, Kristmenn, Krossmenn?*

This was the setting.

Now here is the story.

One year in the Middle '60s, four St. Olaf students and one long-haired hippie-type professor who wore sandals without socks, had a goatee, didn't go to Chapel and got his way paid for free, went on a J-Term* to York, the Old Viking dig, in England.

---

* J-term: This little study interval that the students took in January was instilled when the powers-that-were buckled under to pressures put on them by who knows who.

They were going to study "Peas and Their Impact on Early Viking Life as it Relates to Twentieth Century Norwegian-Lutheran Church Basement Recipes." Two of the students, Ole Nelson and Nels Olson *(not related)*, were Pre-Med turned Philosophy majors, one Forrest Adams Hill III was a Pre-law turned Political Science major, and one Einar Ingram Johnson wanted to major in Economics but he didn't have the Nerve to declare his major because his Dad, Wallace, had warned him many times that *1)* "Anything without a practical application is a waste of everyone's time and money," *2)* "If you are going to take classes on 'The Theories of...' you might as well go to Vo-Tech and take something real," *3)* "Work doesn't count unless it hurts," *4)* "You're only as good as you can Work and just look at all the worthless bankers who only Work part-time and think it's Normal," *5)* "You don't have all your life to sit up on that Hill and dream about Things you can't change anyway," and *6)* "If you get too uppity in your thinking, I'll take you down to Sheldahl's and you can see first-hand for yourself what real Work is all about."

Einar Ingram Johnson had lots to think about, but he was relieved the J-term was in January, the time of year his Dad would be sitting at the dining room Table with his shoeboxes full of tax receipts grumbling about the U.S. Government and preoccupied with what was in front of his nose.

So, on the fourth of January, the four students and the hippie professor who skipped Chapel motored to the Wold-Chamberlain Field in Minneapolis and boarded the airplane bound for England. Einar Johnson was both as nervous and as excited as he could get. He had never seen the Ocean before, much less from an airplane. His Mother, Bernice, who hadn't been right since she got to waltz with Lawrence Welk, had initialed all his underwear and told him to beware of wolves in Sheep's clothing, keep some money in his shoes, and always wear a Scarf around his neck because she had read in some magazine *(she couldn't remember which one)* about a lady who nearly Died from the constant mist that they have in England which can chill a Person to the Bone.

Ole Nelson and Nels Olson, the two Pre-Med turned Philosophy majors who both came from the Suburbs, both had Grandpas who had RR addresses, both had Uncles who were Missionaries Overseas, and both had Great-Grandpas who came from Nor-

Original Spelling

way, also were excited. They had both tried out for the St. Olaf Choir and neither had made it but they didn't have to feel guilty because their Parents hadn't made it either. They decided this was the next best Thing for a chance at seeing some different territory.

Forrest Adam Hill III was neither excited nor nervous. He was from Out East. His Parents, who didn't have a drop of Norwegian blood in them, were divorced. Neither of them had a clue who the Choir Director at St. Olaf was, much less where Northfield was located. His Mother, Charlotte Hestor, an active Member of the Daughters of the American Revolution, read a brochure that Forrest had received in the mail from St. Olaf because he had a high ACT score, and she thought it might be a place that was Homey and quaint because they Served Homemade Rolls. She thought: This is the place for Forrest-

—a kid who is having a tough time. She signed him up both for her Sake and his. Forrest had been to England many times so he was just going for a lack of better Things to do.

As soon as the plane landed in London, the hippie professor who skipped Chapel told the boys he had his own research to do so he would see them in four weeks. The four students were left to fend for themselves. Forrest knew his way around so the rest just followed him. Einar Ingram Johnson had never seen so many People and such a variety in his entire Life. Ole Nelson and Nels Olson, the two who didn't make Choir, had both been to Oslo but found London to be more enticing and exciting. The next Day the four students were supposed to go to York to start their research but Forrest, the one from Out East, suggested they detour to Liverpool to see the Beatles' first stomping ground. All of them agreed. Einar Ingram Johnson thought: Why not, you only Live once. After a couple Days in Liverpool, they made it to York.

In York they got so side-tracked with the pubs, the nightlife, and everything else that wasn't going on in Northfield that

Bastardization

of the

Mother Tongue

they just didn't get down to business to do their research. After living like Prodigal Sons for three and one-half weeks, they headed back to London to meet up with their hippie professor who skipped Chapel. In the train on the way down to London, they brainstormed between pints how they could write their research. Ole Nelson and Nels Olson from the Suburbs thought they could just look up Peas and Vikings in encyclopedias and pull something together on the weekend they got back. But Forrest Adam Hill III had a better idea. He said, for a small fee, he knew a guy Out East who would write the whole Thing. They were all relieved, but Einar Ingram Johnson was feeling some Norwegian guilt for wasting good time and good money. How could he justify *Fram, Fram, Kristmenn, Krossmenn* and have someone else do all his Work? But Einar Ingram Johnson was an innovative thinker and this is why he knew he should be in economics. He thought to himself: I'll just get some County Extension Bulletins about Peas and add a little of my own thoughts and this way, it won't be all wrong.

He also knew he'd feel better when he went Home to visit and show his slides, and his Mom, the Chair of the Local Welk Fan Club, would make him some Cream Peas on Toast.

Split
Peas

&

Other Things That Are Split

15

SPLIT PEAS AND OTHER THINGS THAT ARE SPLIT

Not everything was always harmonious. Before there could be Mergers, there had to be divisions. Just like the Israelites and emigrants from every Valley in Norway, Folks tried to bring over new ideas and to change the status quo. But, like some Peas, things did split. The following are some examples.

Split Peas

West and East Moe

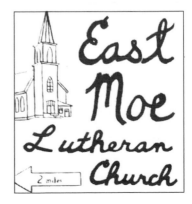

East and West Zion Sang a Hymn Together and Then Simply Split Up

East Zion *(above)*   **West Zion** *(below)*

According to the East and West Zion Lutheran Centennial Book: "In November 1883, Zion Congregation met, sang 'In Jesus Name Shall All Our Work be Done' and calmly split into East Zion and West Zion. Each congregation immediately elected its own officers and made arrangements for dividing joint expenses, but for many years thereafter people referred to East and West Districts, still feeling themselves spiritually one. Pastor Christopher Pederson, identical twin brother of Olaus Pederson, then served a call consisting of *Trefoldigheds* (Trinity, which included Our Savior's and Swenoda) Congregation of Benson, East Zion, and West Zion."

Right—The Green and the Red. No more needs to be said!

Above—Padded and Unpadded Lutheran Church Basement Chairs

Left—Contemporary Lutheran "PK" standing by Renegade-Norwegian-Immigrant-Who-Headed-South Cleng Peerson's Grave in Texas

**East Christiania Cemetery Across the Road from
West Christiania's Cemetery**

Norwegian-Lutheran Church Basement Bars

About As Different As It Gets

Other Things That Are Split

Splittin' Hairs
Grandma Ingeborg
and Grandma Ambjørg

Split Lit

Split End

Split Skirt

Split Personality

Split Second

Split Decision

Splittin' Mad

Splittin' Logs

Split Ticket

Split Rock

Split Level

Splittin' Up

$\mathcal{A}$ "Q & Q" 4 U
$\mathcal{A}$ "Q & $\mathcal{A}$" 4 Others

It's Sunday Night and she's a Corker,
There isn't even a Breeze,
How do you make Hot Food without using the Oven?
You serve Toast under Cream Peas.

16

A "Q & Q" 4 U
A "Q & A" 4 OTHERS

Scandinavians are famous for answering a question with another question.

> Question: "Are you in Town too, then?"
> Response: "Oh, is it you, then?"

Most Scandinavian-American Farm kids had to develop their own answers to Life's questions because grown-ups rarely gave out-and-out answers. Grown-ups just asked a question in return, right?

So that your questions about Cream Peas on Toast can be answered in a way that you understand, the following are some good Question Responses to the 15 Most Common Questions about Peas.

The (small answers in parentheses) indicate how Wesley Methodists, Episcopalians, Presbyterians and some Mission Covenants would reply. Generally, the (small answers in parentheses) would come from Town Folks.

1. CAN YOU PUT PEAS IN A LUNCH BOX?
OF COURSE YOU CAN, BUT WHY WOULD YOU? (Of course you can because they'd fit, but only Chinese and Yuppies eat them raw.)

2. WHAT DOES A NO. 2 CAN OF PEAS MEAN?

WHY WOULD YOU BE SO EXTRAVAGANT AS TO BUY A CAN WHEN YOU CAN CAN YOUR OWN? (Don't worry. No. 2 has nothing to do with eating green Peas and getting the runs.)

3. WHAT CAME FIRST, THE PEA OR THE POD?

WHAT CAME FIRST, THE CHICKEN OR THE EGG? (Nobody has that much free time to sit and think about a question that only God knows the answer to.)

4. HOW MANY PINTS OR QUARTS OF PEAS SHOULD I PUT UP, THEN?

HOW MANY DOINGS ARE YOU GOING TO BE DOING, THEN? (52 pints, and 5 to 6 quarts, depending.*)

---

*48 pints = roughly 1 pint per Sunday for 12 months. *(Most will be for Sunday Nights' Cream Peas on Toast)*

+1 pint to add to the diced carrots at Easter

+1 pint for a Hotdish for the Happy Homemakers' Cooking Demonstration

+2 pints for good measure in case some don't Seal

52 Pints

1 quart for the Mission Festival

1 quart for the Harvest Festival

2 quarts for the Mashed Potatoes on Christmas Eve

1 quart to allow for spoilage

1 quart for a Confirmand, if needed. *(NOTE: If you have twins, or one of your kids is kind of slow, you might have two Confirmands in one year. If you won't be having a Confirmation, you can drop to 5 quarts.)*

6 Quarts (or 5 to 7 depending)

5. HOW LONG SHOULD I SOAK THE PEAS?

HOW MUCH RAIN DOES THE FARMER'S ALMANAC PREDICT FOR YOUR TOWNSHIP THIS YEAR? (Overnight, covered.)

6. WHY DON'T YOU EAT CREAM BEANS ON TOAST?

WHY DON'T YOU WEAR PEDAL-PUSHERS TO CHURCH? (It just doesn't go.)

7. WHY ISN'T PEASANT PRONOUNCED PEAS-ANT?

WHY ISN'T PHEASANT PRONOUNCED FEES-ANT? (Some things just are.)

8. HOW MANY PEAS IN A POD?

HOW BIG IS THE POD? (Just like People, Peas come in different sizes. God loves different sizes, shapes and colors. God loves them all.)

9. WHY ARE THERE SO MANY KINDS OF PEAS?

WHY ARE THERE SO MANY DENOMINATIONS OF LUTHERANS? (Variety is the spice of Life.)

10. WHY DO PEAS PREFER TO GROW IN COLDER CLIMATES?

WHY DO THE NORWEGIANS LIVE IN NORWAY? (They're tough.)

11. WHY AREN'T PEA-NUTS GREEN?

WHY DON'T NORWEGIANS TAN? (It's all in God's color scheme.)

12. WHY DO YOU PUT CREAM PEAS ON TOAST INSTEAD OF ON BREAD?

WHY DID THE PASTOR'S DAUGHTER ALWAYS GET THE PART OF MARY IN THE SUNDAY SCHOOL CHRISTMAS PROGRAM? (These are both Lutheran Standards!)

13. HOW LONG BEFORE YOU RUN OUT OF YOUR SUPPLY OF CANNED PEAS IN YOUR FRUIT CELLAR?

HOW LONG DID IT TAKE YOU TO MEMO-RIZE ALL FIVE PARTS OF LUTHER'S SMALL CAT-ECHISM? (It depends on a lot of things like Doings, size of Family, number of Confirmands, etc.)

14. WHAT IS THE BEST METHOD OF CANNING PEAS: HOT-WATER BATH OR PRESSURE COOKER?

DO YOU HAVE MONEY TO BURN? (Pressure cookers are preferred by Town People who have Fancy Doo-dads and time to watch the gauge.)

15. WHY WAS CREAM PEAS ON TOAST SERVED ON SUNDAY NIGHTS?

WHY CHANGE? (It was a simple way to provide a Hot Meal without too much Fuss on the Lord's Day.)

Well, what do you think of this Q & Q section, then?

CREAM PEAS ON TOAST...
THE FAST FOOD OF THE '40S AND '50S

4-H, Fun, Fellowship

&
Frivolity with Peas

17

4–H, FUN, FELLOWSHIP & FRIVOLITY WITH PEAS

Arlys Arneson, daughter of Axel *(nee Aksel)* and Anna Arneson, was selected to run for the 4–H Talent Queen Contest because her Friends all liked her, she Sewed her own clothes and she was good at Catechization even though she was first because the Pastor always started with the A's.

Arlys had many talents and decided to write and sing a song for the Talent Queen Contest. She was sponsored by the Eager Beavers 4–H Club and by Iverson's Implement whose motto was:

"If she breaks down, we can fix it."

Arlys dedicated this song to her Family and to her 4–H Sewing Project Leader, Ingeborg Ingebretson.

At the contest, Arlys was accompanied by her sister Alane on the Piano. A lot of Relatives and Neighbors came to watch. Arlys was so Down-to-Earth. When she finished singing and before the People clapped, she blushed and told the Crowd, "Please don't think I'm showing off."

She won at the Local Level but was beat out at the Regional Level by someone who wore a strapless and whose Uncle was one of the judges. *(At the Local Level, the Runner-Up was slipping and her Seams were crooked)*.

P. S. Although Arlys didn't win the 4-H Regional Talent Contest, she got to go on to the Tri-County Fair held in Fargo. She had a good time and got a Blue for her Gathered Skirt with a side-zipper.

P. P. S. It was quite a year for the Arnesons because Arlys' 15-year-old brother, Arne, got a Blue for showing his Chester White Boar at the Norman County Fair in Ada. *(His Chester White Boar, Hiriam, grew up eating castaway Pea Shells.)*

Arlys Arneson
COMPOSER AND LOCAL QUEEN

Thing That I Am Thankful For
by Arlys Arneson

I AM THANKFUL FOR SKIES SO BLUE
AND FOR NICE PEOPLE JUST LIKE YOU.
I AM HAPPY WHEN IT RAINS,
AND I HEAR IT ON THE PANES.

(Chorus) BUT THE THING THAT I AM THANKFUL FOR MOST
IS SUNDAY NIGHT WITH CREAM PEAS ON TOAST.

I AM THANKFUL FOR THE FARM,
WHERE NOT A SOUL WOULD DO YOU HARM,
I AM THANKFUL FOR THE SNOW,
IT MAKES SURE THE CROPS WILL GROW.

(Chorus) BUT THE THING THAT I AM THANKFUL FOR MOST
IS SUNDAY NIGHT WITH CREAM PEAS ON TOAST.

I GIVE THANKS FOR MY 4–H CLUB,
MY TALENTS CENTER AROUND ITS HUB.
MY FRIENDS ARE FUN, MY LEADER'S TRUE,
SHE MAKES SURE MY PROJECTS GET BLUE.

(Chorus) BUT THE THING THAT I AM THANKFUL FOR MOST,
IS SUNDAY NIGHT WITH CREAM PEAS ON TOAST.

I AM THANKFUL FOR DAD AND MOM,
AND THAT I CAN RE-USE MY DRESS FROM PROM…
TO BE HERE TONIGHT TO SING TO YOU,
A SONG FROM MY HEART, SO SWEET, SO TRUE.

(Chorus) BUT THE THING THAT I AM THANKFUL FOR MOST,
IS SUNDAY NIGHT WITH CREAM PEAS ON TOAST.

I GIVE THANKS FOR MY CHURCH SO DEAR,
AND FOR BEING LUTHERAN SO I CAN'T HAVE BEER.
I'M THANKFUL THAT MY HEART IS CLEAN,
AND THAT I MIGHT BE CHOSEN YOUR QUEEN.

(Chorus) BUT THE THING THAT I AM THANKFUL FOR MOST,
IS SUNDAY NIGHT WITH CREAM PEAS AND TOAST.

(Add your own verse)

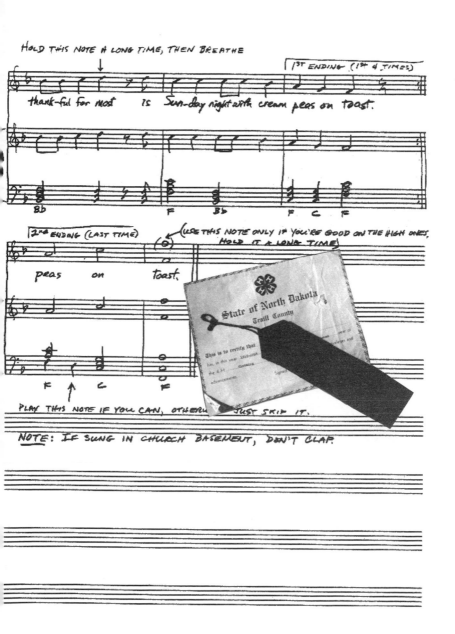

Pea Crafts

Peas are very Versatile vegetables; both Practical and Useful. Peas left over from the year before can still be Useful and used when the New Crop comes in. Making crafts with Dried Peas can be a Wholesome Family Activity, a Rainy Day Project for Clean-Cut kids, a 4–H Project for Achievement Day, or Handy for crafts at VBS or Bible Camp. Designs such as airplanes, Christmas trees, animals, Crosses, etc. can be fitted to any Occasion, if one is just creative.

Here are two samples of Pea Crafts. The rooster is most likely made by an adult who has had some training, and the

pencil box is made by a pupil named Susie. Notice how clever crafters will supplement Pea kernels with beans, corn, Seeds or whatever. *(More craft patterns which teach Conservation Practices for Useful Living and Home Economics can be found in next year's Book from Caragana Press called* Makin' Do.*)*

Another Thing the Family can do is pick someone who is generally quite precise. Call that Person 'It.' Have It count out a big pile of Peas *(Split Peas*

work just fine, either green or yellow) and place them in a Jar. Have the rest of the Family guess how many Peas are in the Jar. The one who comes closest in number is The Winner.

Playhouse Peas

It is best to have the Playhouse in the Woods. Find a little clearing among some Trees. Haul in Old doll Dishes and Grown-Up tea Kettles that have started rusting out. Use a Peach Crate for the Cupboard and Shelf. Stumps make good Chairs and Stools.

Take Rhubarb leaves , ones your Mom is done with, and spread them on the ground for carpet and rugs. If it is late in the Season and the Rhubarb is gone, use the broad leaves from Burdock Plants. Use branches for hanging clothes on, and hang doll blankets over other branches for curtains.

Go to the Caragana Hedge *(usually found between the House and the Barn)* and pick those Fake Pea Pod Things. Sit at the Picnic Table and Shell them. *(See Chapter 6 for the Proper Method.)* Have your doll with you for Company while you Work. You can also use this time to teach her how to Work. *(**Note to Adult Readers:** Don't worry that a young child might actually eat a Caragana Pea Pod. Farm kids know better than that!)*

Caragana is a non-Norwegian, non-English word meaning Pea Tree. Caragana Hedges were planted throughout the Midwest. Caragana Pea Pods made great Playhouse Peas for many kids on many Farms for many years. Hence, the name Caragana Press.

A *Kryssord* for N-LFK's*

ACROSS

1. One of the 4 H's
2. Usually married to Lena
3. Drink of the Viking Gods; Mead
4. Tool for boring holes in Mooringstones
5. Hawaiian Pop Beads
6. Synod that merged with the Augustana Lutheran Church
7. Kind of Cart
8. What Hans Luther Anderson placed in the DECORAH POSTEN *(See Chapter 13)*
9. Variation of Lena's Man
10. *Og* in English
11. Turn _ _ _ _ _ is Fair Play!
12. Who People Liked in '56
13. What Norwegian-Lutherans don't do as far as anyone knows
14. Initials for Norval Kolstad
15. Ingvald Ingvaldson's initials
16. Norse word for beer *(something we only read about!)*
17. What Odin carried
18. Slang for Dad
19. Best non-White Norwegian-Lutheran vegetables
20. Norway's second largest City

DOWN

1. Crown for Confirmed kids
2. Fake Butter
3. Opposite of *ja*
4. Norwegian Christmas Cookie (*Norsk* plural ending)

*Norwegian-Lutheran Farm Kids

5. A Current Synod
6. Double Toothpicks as in HE_ _
7. To _ _, or Not To _ _
8. How many _ _ _ _ _ do I have to tell you?
9. Vessel that holds Hollyhocks
10. What the A in NDAC stood for
11. Location of Douglas County, MN, Fairgrounds
12. *(Ignore this one. It doesn't mean anything, but it's too late to change it).*
13. What you could do in The Lake

Ode to a Pint of Peas

Johan Knutsvig, who had studied J. Keats, was particularly fond of Keats' "Ode on a Grecian Urn."

Knutsvig wrote this poem when he was 86 years old and residing in the Rest O'er the Hill Nursing Home. He wrote this on Tuesday when there wasn't anything to do because the Workmen were painting the shuffleboard court, and then of course, the volunteer barber wasn't coming until Thursday and Johan's roommate, Ole Grindal, was a little Under The Weather so Knutsvig had no one to talk to. Still, it was a nice June Day and Johan was left alone with his thoughts of Yesterday and Memories of Days Gone By and of course, Peas were right up there.

Although he had studied Keats, deep down Johan Knutsvig really felt that if someone was going to waste time writing down frivolous Stuff and calling it poetry, one should at least make it rhyme and tell it like it is. No double talk, no double meanings, no slang and no interpretation should be necessary.

P.eaS. It had been two years since His Wife, Clara Helene *(Larsdottir from Numedal)* had Passed On.

ODE TO A PINT OF PEAS

by Johan Knutsvig

(This might bring tears to your eyes.)

WHEN I THINK BACK ON THE GARDEN PLOT,
I THINK OF PEAS, AND WE PICKED A LOT.

WE PICKED AND SHUCKED 'TIL THE SUN ROSE HIGH,
AND MA CALLED, "DINNER, THERE'S RHUBARB PIE!"

WE ALL SAT DOWN AND WE ALL SAID GRACE,
AND ASKED FOR BLESSINGS, JUST IN CASE...

THE RAIN DIDN'T COME AND THE DROUGHT HELD OUT,
AND THE CROPS DRIED UP, BUT WE WOULDN'T DOUBT...

OUR FAITH WAS SURE, OUR BELIEFS *(Lutheran)* WERE STRAIGHT,
IF THERE WAS NO RAIN, THAT WAS OUR FATE.

WE'D ACCEPT OUR BURDEN, OUR CROSS TO BEAR,
IF THERE WASN'T ENOUGH, WE'D ALWAYS SHARE.

WE'D SIT ON THE PEW LIKE PEAS IN A POD,
AND THINK GOOD THOUGHTS AND PRAISE OUR GOD.

H	A	N	D	S		O	L	E
A	L	E		A	W	L		L
L	E	I		N		E	L	C
O	X		A	D		O	L	A
	A			B				
A	N	D		A	B	O	U	T
	D		I	K	E			I
D	R	I	N	K		V		M
I	I		Ø	L		A	X	E
P	A		P	E	A	S		S
		B	E	R	G	E	N	

Answers to *Kryssord* Puzzle on page 147

*Interviews
about
Cream Peas Toast*

Think of all the Starving kids in China!

18

INTERVIEWS ABOUT CREAM PEAS ON TOAST

I t's hard to find someone who doesn't like Cream Peas on Toast. Here are some typical reactions to these two Earth-shaking questions: 1) Have you ever had Cream Peas on Toast, 2) Do you like it?

Per *(Man of Few Words)* Persson

- Have you ever had Cream Peas on Toast? —*Ja.*
- Do you like it? —*Ja.*

Per and Clement

Clement Clemmenson

- Have you ever had Cream Peas on Toast? —Oh, for sure.
- Do you like it? —Oh, so much, *ja.*

> EAT! YOU'VE GOT TO KEEP YOUR STRENGTH UP!

Fern, Olga and Norman

Fern Fedje
- Have you ever had Cream Peas on Toast? —Several times.
- Do you like it?
    —I like Cream Peas for Decoration Day the best.

Olga Urness
- Have you ever had Cream Peas on Toast?
    —Well, of course. I wasn't born Yesterday.
- Do you like it?   —Well, of course. I'm no fool.

Norman Nestuen
- Have you ever had Cream Peas on Toast?
    —What do you think?
- Do you like it?   —Doesn't everybody?

WE DIDN'T HAVE DEPRESSION GLASS. WE HAD DEPRESSION DISHES: CREAM MUSH, MILK MUSH, WHITE MACARONI, CREAM ON BREAD AND CREAM PEAS ON TOAST.

Inga Ingebritsson

• Have you ever had Cream Peas on Toast?

—Ja, mange ganger.

• Do you like it?

—Ja, meget godt.

Mr. and Mrs. Ingebritsson

Einar Ingebritsson

• Have you ever had Cream Peas on Toast?

—Ja, her i Amerika.

• Do you like it?

—Det beste er godt nok.

Sigurd Swenson

- Have you ever had Cream Peas on Toast?

  —*Ja,* you betcha.

- Do you like it?   —*Ja,* you betcha.

Sigurd, the Scyther, Sire, Sigher

Jens and The Wife

Jens Karlsrud

- Have you ever had Cream Peas on Toast?   —Yes.
- Do you like it?   —Yup.

Mrs. Jens Karlsrud

- Have you ever had Cream Peas on Toast?

  —*Ja,* whenever I need it.

- Do you like it?   —It makes me really Comfortable.

Myrtle
and
Alice

Myrtle Sanstead

• Have you ever had Cream Peas on Toast?
—Yes, most certainly.
• Do you like it?
—It's my favorite. When my whole Family is here, I open up five Jars and that's no lie. Erik eats it any way, Hot or cold, Plain or on Toast.

Alice Borgrud

• Have you ever had Cream Peas on Toast?
—*Ja,* but not for a long time.
• Do you like it? —It's mighty good.

Modern Times

When You Might Need Comfort Food

19

MODERN TIMES WHEN YOU MIGHT NEED COMFORT FOOD

There are many times in this Day and Age when you long for a Simpler Life and wish you were back in the Days before Melmac and Bonanza. Back to the Days of White Dishes and Ma Perkins and 'CCO's Farm Report. At times like this, it is okay to go Home from Work and have Cream Peas on Toast for Supper. To get over an especially tough Day, top it off with a Bowl of either Rhubarb Sauce or Purple Plum Sauce.

Here are some times when you might need the Comfort that can only be found in a quiet Meal of Cream Peas on Toast:

- It is April 14 of any year and your taxes aren't done yet.
- It's been 25 years since The Men walked on the moon and you haven't even been to Yellowstone yet.
- You took the kids to a Family wedding on your Mother's side and they behaved like a bunch of heathens.
- Your boss says downsizing and re-engineering are more than passing fads.
- The transmission goes out on your wife's car the week after you gave the Church Offering a little extra.

- It dawns on you that when your kids say they are going to hang out they aren't volunteering to help with The Wash.
- The only channel that comes in is MTV.
- You're daughter is living in sin " 'cuz everyone else is doing it" and she doesn't give a rip which Aunts know about it.
- Now that you have mastered it, you get notified that the Family Financial Aid Application for college has been revised again.
- Your Pick-Up gets recalled for emissions control flaws.
- You realize your boss, your doctor, your Neighbor who has had three bypasses and the President of the United States are all younger than you.
- You visit your Mother in the Nursing Home and she again asks to visit the Old Homeplace that you sold to the DNR in 1988 for Wetland Reclamation and tuition money.
- Your son met a girl when he was in the Military and she doesn't even know what To Turn means.
- You Worked real hard to keep it to yourself when your daughter decided to marry a Catholic from The Cities and now your cousin's daughter who was in VISTA is planning to marry a Hindu from India and all his Relatives are coming for the wedding at the Country Church. Where do you put them all up, then?
- Wal-Mart is coming to town, the Sears store is closing, and you still remember Roebuck.
- When everything you read and hear is about the global economy and you're still trying to figure out what the signs "Modern Housekeeping" at resorts mean.
- You struggled to learn to diagram sentences and now your kids are saying "he goes and she goes and they go" when they really mean "he said and she said…"

- You hear talk that the Hymnal might be revised again.

- Your colored wedding picture on the Living Room wall is fading and you haven't even paid off the Mortgage yet.

- You've been a Faithful Member of Our Saviour's Lutheran for 45 years and now they are talking about starting a Contemporary Service.

- Jell-O comes out with a new flavor that looks just like Mrs. Stewart's Bluing.

- Your son-in-law, the agronomist in The Cities, asks if you've picked out your Cemetery plot yet.

- The School District wants money to "go interactive" and to develop a multimedia center and you still remember Party Lines and Rubbernecking.

- Your 8th grader wants to wear a tee shirt with the Queen of Spades on it to the Family Reunion.

- Your husband says it is okay for your daughter to go to a rock concert and you couldn't even go to the Sadie Hawkins dance because you weren't Confirmed yet.

- You have to mow the lawn before the Confirmation Party but the Weather just won't cooperate.

- You find yourself spending more time developing Mission Statements than attending Mission Suppers.

- More and more you find yourself asking, "Is nothing Sacred anymore?"

WHAT WILL SOOTHE IT ALL?

CREAM PEAS ON TOAST, THAT'S FOR SURE!

There is one other time when only Cream Peas on Toast will do:

When your daughter gets engaged to a nice Norwegian-Lutheran boy from the Country and you know it was all worth the struggle and that Things are finally Turning Out as they should!

Mr. and Mrs. Theodore T. Johnson
request the honour of your presence
at the marriage of their daughter
Suzann
to
Mr. Ronald E. Nelson
on Sunday, the nineteenth of March
Nineteen hundred and sixty-seven
at four o'clock in the afternoon
☙
Den Norske Lutherske Mindekirke
East 21st Street and 10th Avenue South
Minneapolis, Minnesota

Reception following ceremony
in church basement

Ei Gammel Kransekake

The Caragana Characters

About the Authors

20

THE
CARAGANA CHARACTERS

About the Authors

Peas in a Pod: A Special Variety

These two full-blooded Norwegian women from Rural areas were born in the same month in the same year and met at the same college on the same day. They both lived on second floor of Gerda Mortensen Hall at Augsburg College. They had both attended Our Saviour's Lutheran as girls growing up *(same name, different congregations)*, both had Grandfathers named Tollef *(different men)*, and both eventually married full-blooded Scandinavian-Lutheran boys *(different ones)* from Rural areas.

At Augsburg College, they each majored in foreign languages that both began with S: one in Spanish, and the other in Scandinavian Studies. They both became mothers to all girls, and both live in split levels in small cities that have the Mississippi running right through the middle. *(Even though the counters look pretty gaudy, both still have White kitchen countertops with gold glittery flecks in them. They'll replace them when the counters wear out. They're both still perfectly good counters!)*

While it seems the authors share a brain, their youngest daughters—both born in 1974—share a middle name, Elise, after their great-grandmothers *(not the same woman, though)*. Both of these daughters spent time at the Concordia Language Villages *(same village, but different times)*. The Caragana Characters' oldest daughters, Jen and Sen, were both born in 1969 and had their first homes in the Franklin/Riverside area of Minneapolis.

Right after their liberal training at Augsburg College, Janet and Suzann both became a little more ecumenical. You see, they took the same childbirth classes at the same time, but these classes were at a Catholic hospital in Minneapolis. *(They figured it was okay though, because the hospital wasn't far from Augsburg.)* They both agree that these classes, unlike so many they had taken at Augsburg together, were completely worthless. Really, what first-hand experience do nuns have with childbirth?

Janet and Suzann's middle names are their mothers' first names, and each has a brother with their fathers' names for a middle name. Both prefer melted Butter on their *lutefisk* rather than White Sauce. "Save the White Sauce for the Peas," they say. If any Sugar at all, they use White Sugar on their *lefse* rather than brown. Both say pana-cakes instead of pancakes and both grew up learning *"Ride, Ride Ranken," "I Jesu Navn,"* and to count in Norwegian.

Of course, both took piano lessons and accompanied the Sunday School Singers, and both were in piano recitals. One of them boasts of playing the Minute Waltz in two minutes and forty-five seconds flat at one recital. *(A Neighbor lady timed her.)* The other Caragana Character used to play six-hand piano with her two sisters. *(All three shared one bench.)*

Both took baton lessons, and both were in The Band. Both had blue and White high school colors although neither had ever seen or heard of a blue and White tiger or a blue and white burro, their school mascots.

Although both grew up on farms, neither has ever Milked a Cow—probably because they each had brothers. To this day, neither wears shoes anymore than necessary, no matter what the season, temperature or terrain.

Both were Baptized into the Lutheran Faith in November 1946 and both reaffirmed their Baptismal vows in May 1961. Of course, in honor of that event, both wore White Gowns and White Shoes, had red carnations, and both received Bulova watches from their Parents. Both of their Fathers thought their "girls looked pretty spiffy that day." Their moms just cooked for the Confirmation Company. Of course, both had been the first in their respective classes to memorize all of LUTHER'S SMALL CATECHISM and recite it for the minister. Their Mothers had called these sessions Confirmation Classes, but their Fathers called them Reading for the Minister, something both Fathers had done in the Norwegian language.

Both grew up in Homes where face cards were generally frowned upon. Neither of them were allowed to, and therefore neither of them ever learned, to dance. Both have been known to try to Two-Step with their husbands, but they agree that it just seems so "show-offy and awkward." They prefer to sit and visit. Both can make just about anything except clothing out of Rhubarb!

Their husbands, too, have a great deal in Common besides a similar Heritage, Common religion and Upbringing. Both men have Relatives who are Free-ers today, and both men were student teachers—a humbling experience for already quiet Folks. Even though both men now Work for The Government, they are still Good People and let their wives take the limelight.

Both men were born in March. Of course, it goes without saying, that this is the first marriage for all four of them: Janet and Neil, Suzann and Ron. Three of these four hailed from the Red River Valley Area, but the other came from the Kensington Runestone Area. Suzann and Ron were married on Neil's birthday but they didn't know it—or him—at that time.

Naturally, both of the Caragana Characters had Playhouses in the Woods and Caragana Hedges on the Farms where they grew up.

Split Peas: A Special Variety

In some ways, the Caragana Characters are Split Peas too: one belonged to the YDFL and Scandinavian Club on campus, and the other belonged to the YGOP and Spanish Club. One lived in Zeta House, and the other in Iota House.

One came from a Family of seven, and one came from a Family of three. One came from a Farmers' Union background and the other had a Farm Bureau Upbringing. One campaigned for Barry Goldwater on the streets of Minneapolis while the other attended Bean Feeds for Hubert Humphrey at the St. Paul Fairgrounds.

Although both articles of clothing had side-zippers, one made her first Gathered Full Skirt for 4–H and the other made hers in Home Ec.

While both had to read THE POPULATION DILEMMA during the Summer of '64 as mandated for orientation by Augsburg authorities, one took the Book's plot to heart and stopped with two children. The other apparently didn't, and had three children. Janet says, "Even though Sarah isn't named after anyone Special, she still looks Norwegian!"

In high school, both attended Concordia Days in Moorhead, Minnesota, but they attended different Bible Camps: one went to Luther Crest near Alexandria, Minnesota, and the other to Red Willow Bible Camp in Binford, North Dakota. One went to both the Luther League Conventions in Miami and Detroit, but the other was sent by her Minister to Lutheran Bible Institute in Seattle for a week so she wouldn't get exposed to undesirable elements or thoughts at the Conventions. Both heard Nelson Trout throughout their Luther League careers. While one has fond Luther League Memories of Hymn 550 in The Red Hymnal, the other prefers #141 in YOUTH SINGS.

During one of their dates in their Courtin' Days, Suzann and Ron went to a grocery store and bought Bread, Cream and Karo Syrup and went to Ron's apartment for a wonderful Dinner and Evening. They feel that the Evening and the Cream and Bread sort of cemented their future together. On the other hand, due to a lack of finances but with a wealth of Tradition, Janet just made do and prepared Cream Peas on Toast for Neil for one of their first Married Meals. She says, "It wasn't so good, but he didn't seem to mind. He didn't say anything."

In other examples of their splitness—known to Episcopalians as individuality—one has blond hair and a round face and prefers the Cream, and the other has dark hair, a thin face and prefers the Peas.

Janet Letnes Martin, daughter of the late John and Helen Klemetson Letnes, grew up in the rural setting of Hillsboro, ND. Both her maternal and paternal grandparents came from Norway and helped settle the Hillsboro area. She received her B.A. from Augsburg College in Minneapolis and furthered her studies at the University of Minnesota.

In 1983, Janet wrote a family history book entitled REISTE TIL AMERIKA. She has co-authored three books—CREAM AND BREAD, SECOND HELPINGS OF CREAM AND BREAD, and LUTHERAN CHURCH BASEMENT WOMEN: LUTEFISK, LEFSE, LUNCH AND JELL-O—with Allen Todnem of Hastings, Minnesota. She also wrote SHIRLEY HOLMQUIST AND AUNT

WILMA: WHO DUNIT? and is the creator of HELGA'S HOTFLASH HANKYS. She averages one hundred speaking engagements per year.

She resides in Hastings, Minnesota, with her husband, Neil Martin, who grew up in Newfolden, Minnesota. They have three Scandinavian-Lutheran daughters: Jennifer, Sarah, and Katrina.

Suzann Nelson says she has several sections in her brain roughly divided into Norwegian, Nerd-dom and Nonsense, and that each section holds predominance for about 10 to 12 years. After graduating from high school in Evansville, Minnesota, she attended and graduated from Augsburg College. She also did considerable graduate work at the University of Oslo and the University of Minnesota.

She directed *Skogfjorden,* Concordia College's Norwegian Language Village in the '70s, and the Northern Minnesota Citizens League in the '80's and early '90s. Although she has authored many public policy reports and position papers as an elected official and as director of the League and has written many language curricula, this is the first un-Nerdy thing she has written. She says that the Nerd-dom section of her brain is being overtaken by a convergence of the Norwegian and Nonsense sections. She finds it a very liberating experience and plans to write a lot more for fun, therapy and money!

She and her husband, Ron—singer, composer, government employee and native of Portland, North Dakota—are the parents of two Wholesome 100-percent Pure Norwegian-American-Lutheran daughters, Senja and Siri. They live in Grand Rapids, Minnesota.

Although the Caragana Characters kept in contact with

each other throughout the '70s and '80s by sporadic phone calls to tell crazy stories and by sending each other Family Christmas Pictures, they didn't realize how much they shared a brain until the Summer of 1994 when they decided to team up and make some money to get those five girls through college.

The Caragana Characters' plans include several more publications including a They-We Series: THEY HAD STORES AND WE HAD CHORES, a Town/Country Lexicon; and THEY GLORIFIED MARY AND WE GLORIFIED RICE, a Catholic/ Lutheran Lexicon. There are at least three more Books in the workings of their brain/s and kitchen Tables.

Both are saddened by the tremendous growth in numbers of People who wish they were Norwegian-Lutherans. As an accommodation to those People, and as part of Janet and Suzann's Obligatory Mission Work, they are planning to form a Norwegian-Lutheran Wannabe Club. Membership dues will be low, but members' standards will be high.

For further information on the club, to relate a story, to book them for a program, or to get on the Caragana, Redbird, Sentel or Martin House mailing lists, write to:

The Caragana Characters
Box 396
Hastings, MN 55033

ORDER FORM
for
CREAM PEAS ON TOAST

Name _____

Address _____

City _____ State _____ Zip _____

No. of copies_____ @ $9.95   **Subtotal:** $ _____

Plus postage & handling (per book)

      1st Class $3.00 per book $ _____

      Book Rate $1.50 per book $ _____

(Maximum postage cost for multiple orders: $6.00)

MN Residents add 6.5% Sales Tax $ _____

                      TOTAL: $ _____

Send cash, check or money order to:

    CARAGANA PRESS

    Box 396

    Hastings, MN 55033

FOR COPIES OF OTHER BOOKS co-authored by Janet Letnes Martin and for HELGA'S HOTFLASH HANKY orders and copies of SHIRLEY HOLMQUIST AND AUNT WILMA: WHO DUNIT?, write to:

    Martin House Productions

    Box 274

    Hastings, MN 55033

Other books co-authored by Martin with Al Todnem:

- CREAM AND BREAD
- SECOND HELPINGS OF CREAM AND BREAD
- LUTHERAN CHURCH BASEMENT WOMEN:
  - LUTEFISK LEFSE, LUNCH AND JELL-O